For Cousins Bud and Pat

Good to have the time together.
Thanks for coming to Portland.
Some desperation reading for
a cold winter evening.

Love,
Cousin Earl
July 9, 2003

Lawrence F. Small, Ph.D (1925 –)
is also the author of:

*Trails Revisited: The Story of the Montana-Northern Wyoming
Conference of the United Church of Christ*

A Century of Politics on the Yellowstone

Journey with the Law: The Life of William J. Jameson

Montana Passage: A Homesteader's Heritage

Pryor Mountain Press, Billings, MT 59102
© Pryor Mountain Press
Rocky Mountain College
1511 Poly Drive, Billings, MT 59102
All rights reserved. Published 2002
Printed in the United States of America

1 3 5 7 9 10 8 6 4 2

ISBN 0-9722984-0-1

This book is printed on acid-free paper.
Set in Berkeley and Isadora

Designed by Stacie French

Courageous Journey

The Road to
Rocky Mountain College

Lawrence F. Small

Pryor Mountain Press
Rocky Mountain College
Billings, Montana

Alpha Literary Society, 1914

Courage is the most basic of the virtues,

because it is the one that guarantees

all the others. — *Winston Churchill*

Pioneer Literary Society, 1914

For the trailmakers
of the open door to learning;
those of irrepressible hope and good will—
distant voices that echo across the years.

Prescott Hall, built in 1916, was used for meals and social life.

CONTENTS ✜

PREFACE ▓

This study stems in good part from conversations over the years with graduates of Rocky Mountain's predecessor institutions. There were a few contacts early on with the College of Montana, and more with Wesleyan, Intermountain Union, and the Polytechnic Institute. Mostly, there were memories of proud if struggling schools, enduring gratitude for an open door to learning, for friendships that enriched, and for teachers who really mattered. If the way was uphill for those who dreamed and persevered, it led at last to an institution in Billings which the students wisely named Rocky Mountain College.

It would be presumptuous to more than survey the stories of the six schools leading to the merger of 1947. For those with a more intimate knowledge—alumni, teachers, others—of one or more of the institutions, this account may miss more than it reports. The historian's lens is too limited to capture the finer details that matter as readers recall their yesterdays. Similarly, the writer risks the sin of omission in acknowledging those who have been helpful in preparing this volume.

Libraries and their archives provided an indispensable resource and deep appreciation is extended to the following: Montana Historical Society Library, Conrad Kohrs Memorial Library (Deer Lodge), Parmly Billings Library (Montana Room), Presbyterian Historical Library (Philadelphia), Methodist and Rocky Mountain College Archives. For access to the last, appreciation is expressed to Joyce Jensen (Methodist archivist) and Librarian Jan Jelinek and staff.

The search for primary sources benefited greatly from Prof. Robert Lyon's research notes from an earlier study of the predecessor schools. L. Thomas Eaton, son of Lewis and Mary Eaton, shared his collection of papers on the Montana College and the Polytechnic Institute. Harley O'Donnell made available some of his grandfather's (I.D. O'Donnell) memorabilia and Prof. Carroll Van West sent information on the James J. Hill gift of land. Ann Ferguson assisted with data on President Wendell Brook's later career and Vava Van de Mark Johnstone provided background on President Jesse Bunch, her parents' lifelong friend.

Edna Nutter of Shelby shared perspectives from her years at Intermountain Union. Her editions of *The Nuttercracker*, a notable "labor of love" featured in Rocky publications like *The Monitor,* carried news of graduates of the four predecessor schools. Harriett C. Meloy of Helena provided insights into Intermountain's short stay in Great Falls. Dr. Scott Pennepacker of Missoula and sister Pennie Coombs of Billings reflected on their father's time as Dean of Polytechnic-Intermountain. Time limited the interview process, but included helpful sessions with Clara Klindt, Otis Hopper, and Frank and Helen Matthew.

Wesleyan and Intermountain Union's *Prickly Pear* and the Polytechnic's *Poly* were valuable resources, both for the photographic record and the written word. If the times were often lean, these annuals hardly took notice as they pictured a campus life full of purpose and activity— in all, something of the best four years to be found in a student's life.

The preparation of the manuscript for the printer was ably handled by Cindy Kunz, Administrator of the Institute for Peace Studies at Rocky Mountain College, with photo processing by Jan Jelinek and student assistants Lana Anderson and Faye Pegan at the Educational Resource Center. I am deeply indebted to them. I am also grateful for President Arthur DeRosier's review and suggestions for the manuscript as well as for his Introduction. His interest and the authorization of the College's Board of Trustees made this study possible. My thanks, also, to Dr. Susan McDaniel, Vice President for Academic Affairs at Rocky, for reviewing the manuscript, and to Victoria Cech, Director of Grants at Rocky Mountain College, and Stacie French, graphic design artist, for preparing the manuscript for publication. Finally, as with previous publications, I express appreciation to my wife Elfie for her understanding and encouragement of the author's task.

Lawrence F. Small
Billings, Montana
May, 2002

INTRODUCTION ❦

It has been said that no nation can be any better than the education system it provides its citizens, and that a mind is a terrible thing to waste, and that the pen is mightier than the sword. On and on go the tributes to learning, and they are important to contemplate. However, what is more important is the fact that we Americans really believe these sayings, and our national consciousness includes the belief that our past growth, current prosperity, and future well being is tied up in an education system that begins around age five and continues through twelve years of grade and high school and then college years, be it two at a community college, four at a private or public baccalaureate institution, or more at the masters and even doctoral level. We believe in the importance of learning, even if we home school, and we shudder to think of educational erosion, if, indeed, there is erosion. There are always among us naysayers and prophets of doom, but as a nation we are ever on our guard lest erosion actually takes place. So long as we remain involved and vigilant, we shall strengthen, diversify, and perpetuate quality education on both the private and public level, but it will erode if involvement gives way to self-satisfaction, lost objectivity, and, worst of all, conscious neglect.

As the nation took shape, first in thirteen north-to-south East Coast colonies, and, then, westward to the Pacific shores and beyond, I have always found it fascinating to see how soon schools were put in place. On the East Coast schools were public in the north, parochial in the middle states, and tutorial in the south .... No matter: they were there. Massachusetts Bay Colony was born in 1630; Harvard College was founded in 1636. As folks moved west, schools appeared as soon as barns and homes were erected and crops planted. Children spent the four non-planting, chopping, or harvesting months in school, and they were expected to absorb as much in that time frame as they might in nine months. Learning was not to be neglected, and those small, semi-barren, mostly rural schools performed wonders not yet heralded in the history of our nation.

Schools were built, elementary education was required, high school possibilities followed (mostly after the Civil War), and denominations galore founded four-year undergraduate colleges that gave definition to progress American style. What a galaxy of names these colleges form: what a difference they have made in our history and our heritage. They, in many ways, formed the America we know and enjoy today. The Congregationalists, Methodists, Lutherans, Baptists, Catholics, Mormons, Presbyterians, and so many more put down educational stakes and rang the college school bell for all to hear and heed. Many colleges were born and soon died. Some were born, glowed for a bit, and, then, died. Some are hundreds of years old and are still with us today— important, applauded examples of Man's desire to learn, achieve and contribute. Their history is a glorious page in our national chapter of contributions to Mankind. That page is to be applauded as much as any other in that chapter.

I am told that cats have nine lives. I will buy that scientific (or non-scientific) conclusion. If so, some colleges do, too. One of the great college birth-to-success stories is recorded in this volume. It is the story of Montana Collegiate Institute, or is it The College of Montana, or Montana Wesleyan University, or Intermountain Union College, or Billings Polytechnic Institute, or Lord knows what else. It is an often named and renamed college that has had many lives, and has looked death in the face more times than a cat and somehow came away bloodied but alive to fight another day.

There were recessions, depressions, droughts, earthquakes, financial no shows, wars (at least three major ones), and grasshoppers, but none— singularly or in combination—could administer the knockout punch. It is a college meant to live and contribute, and today it stands as the oldest continuing business in Montana, and a monument to Territorial settlers who wanted a college in place eleven years before statehood. What gall; what swagger and pretentiousness. How could a college formed in a Territory without direction and light years away from the center of things (whatever that means) hope for a natural birth in 1878 and a life of service through the growth of an infant nation into a world power when all of the above mentioned names gave way finally to one name—Rocky Mountain College—in 1947. That story of faith and vision, gall and cockiness, hope, failure, and more hope is penned with expertness by Lawrence Small, who has lived with predecessors he admires and whose hopes he has shared lo these many years while this fine history has been in production. It begins at the beginning (1878) and ends in 1947, when three denominations came together to create a united Rocky Mountain College. Professor Small lays the groundwork for the RMC story, but he also lifts our consciousness, buoys our spirits, and defines what is possible in education when defeated leaders ignore defeat and live to create a college that produces leaders in myriad fields year after year. If hope is your bag, you will enjoy this story. If tenaciousness is your partner, you will soar with those heroes long dead. If joy in seeing success leapfrog defeat is what challenges and elevates your spirit, you will enjoy this volume authored by one who brings life to leaders long buried and forgotten. May their contributions live forever in the life of a good college getting better daily.

Arthur H. DeRosier, Jr., *President*
Rocky Mountain College
May, 2002

PROLOGUE: ❈ 1877

For the young territory the new year seemed to signal better times to come. The population was growing, following the depression of 1873, and would soon surge with developments in mining and agriculture and the arrival of the railroads, with all that they would mean to the economy and to life in general. The notable increase in women and children since the Census of 1870 indicated a more settled citizenry.

On the political scene, Territorial Governor Benjamin F. Potts, in office since 1870, was providing the first strong leadership, meeting lingering Civil War passion with a spirit of compromise and conciliation. His much-needed reforms in territorial finances made for a healthier climate for business and investment. Government benefited from his insistence upon competence in public office, as he removed the dishonest and the incapable, while appointing men of the stature of Cornelius Hedges as Superintendent of Public Instruction.

Schools had appeared early for the few children in the mining camps, first as subscription affairs where the parents paid for instruction. In 1865 the new territorial legislature adopted a school law, authorizing county commissioners to establish local school districts and impose a one-mill levy to support public education. The first public school opened at Virginia City in March of 1866. Granville Stuart remembered how cattle companies also encouraged schooling by providing a log house and teacher for a six-months' term. He added that the young woman teacher would be equipped with a good saddle horse "and plenty of cowboy attention to stave off loneliness." [1]

By 1870, the territory had only 15 public schools, enrolling some 1,350 students, with 27 teachers and a total expenditure of approximately $12,000. Hedges brought to a daunting task the firm conviction of his New England breeding concerning the importance of learning, fortified with degrees from Yale and Harvard. During his tenure in office, four terms in all, he worked energetically and innovatively to lengthen the school year, encourage regular attendance, improve the curriculum, secure greater financing, provide teacher training—in all to richly merit the title of "Father of Education in Montana." [2]

His advocacy of "summer normal schools" to promote standards and improve teaching had to suffice in the absence of colleges, and he was gratified with legislative approval in 1877. In the Constitutional Convention of 1884, Hedges would help to compose an Education Article which provided for a university system. Congress was not receptive to statehood for Montana at that time, but the Article was adopted in large part in the later document of 1889.

Meanwhile, others were voicing concern for an educated citizenry, including the desire for colleges closer to home. Church leaders, among others, were not unaware of the advance of denominational schools westward, despite the growth of new state universities. Congregationalism, for instance, following the Civil War, was penetrating the prairie and mountain regions with colleges in Kansas, Minnesota, Colorado, Nebraska, South Dakota, and Washington. [3]

In Montana, it was the Methodists in 1877 who first expressed an interest in a "school of higher learning." Meeting in Bozeman in early August, in the first session of the Montana Annual Conference, a handful of preachers and laity resolved:

> The Educational interests of Montana demand immediate action on the part of our Church in the establishment of a school of a higher grade to meet the wants of our people who are unable to bear the expense of sending their children to Eastern schools. [4]

Along with the cost of distant learning, the Conference worried about "Romish" influences on the young, admonishing parents not to send their children to convent schools. Feelings ran deeply and figured prominently in the resolve to have an institution along denominational principles.

But it was bold talk lacking substance considering the few Methodists in Montana at that time, shepherded by only four full-fledged preachers serving far-flung circuits. President Grant's "Quaker Policy" had added responsibilities for them on Indian reservations. Nevertheless, a committee was appointed "to take such measures as they shall think best toward the establishment of a school at one of the principal points in the Territory."

Named to the committee were Governor Benjamin F. Potts, Reverend Francis Asbury Riggin (two college degrees), Reverend Clark Wright (future Superintendent of Public Instruction), W. W. Alderson, and William Wesley Van Orsdel. The last mentioned, Methodism's beloved "Brother Van," though unlettered, would be a major force behind Montana Wesleyan.

The Bozeman group was grateful for the presence of their bishop, for there had been fear that he might encounter Chief Joseph and the Nez Perce on their flight that summer to Canada. But Reverend Thomas Bowman had made it safely from Denver, in time to preside over the little gathering in the church on Olive Street. He endorsed the interest in a school of higher learning: it was in keeping with Methodism's mission in the West. Nothing happened, however, and then another committee was formed in 1882, followed by still another authorized to choose a school site. Finally, at the Missoula Conference in 1888 action was taken to start a college in Helena.

Elsewhere, in 1877, a similar sentiment was building for educational opportunities closer to home. In Deer Lodge, it was men such as Edwin H. Irvine who led the way. His daughter later recalled:

> In the year 1877 my father, Edwin H. Irvine, who was a college graduate and appreciated the value of higher education, was faced with the problem of how to secure this education for his seven children. There were other heads of families in Deer Lodge and all over the Territory of Montana who were considering the same problem. The only educational institution in the territory, aside from the public school, was a Catholic convent. Some people were sending their girls there for a finishing course—but many Protestants, of whom my father was one, feared the Catholic influence. A few sent their children to eastern colleges, but this was very expensive and due to a lack of railroads seemed very far away.[5]

Irvine was a Kentucky native, an 1857 graduate of Bethany College in West Virginia, whose family had relocated to Missouri. The destruction of their prosperous farms during the Civil War had prompted a move to the Deer Lodge Valley in 1866. In addition to farming, he was involved in profitable gold mining water supply projects. His interest in a college was shared by others in town; prominent men such as William Andrews Clark, Conrad Kohrs, and Judge Hiram Knowles, and he proceeded to organize efforts which would lead to the opening of the Montana Collegiate Institute the following year.

It was the Irvines that James Bryce depicted in his classic work, *The American Commonwealth*, when he spoke of those in "the rural districts of the country" who "set learning in visible form, plain, indeed, and humble, but dignified even in her humility, before the eyes of rustic people, in whom the love of knowledge, naturally strong, might never break from the bud into the flower but for the care of some zealous gardener." Writing in 1888, the famed British historian and statesman found much to admire in some of the "smaller Western colleges, " where "men of great ability and great attainment" served "students who are receiving an education quite as thorough, though not always as wide, as the best Eastern universities can give." [6]

The beginnings were indeed "humble" that summer of 1877, whether at Bozeman or at Deer Lodge, with years of unrelenting struggle to come, but there was a measure of prophecy in the eminent Britisher's words, as able teachers with a compelling desire to serve and students with an eagerness for learning found their way to Deer Lodge, to Helena, and to the Polytechnic Institute in the river town of Billings.

In all, six schools would share in a story that continues today in the life of Rocky Mountain College. Each has its own annals, brief in cases, but what makes their history an uncommon one in American higher education is the inscrutable way in which paths converged in the creation of an ecumenically-fashioned school in Billings. From a legacy of diverse parentage of once proud colleges, Rocky Mountain derives strength for the years ahead.

PART ONE

❖

COLLEGE OF MONTANA

Seedtime in Deer Lodge
College of Montana
Montana College

Rev. Wiley Mountjoy, Local Disciples Minister, operated the interim school at the Institute

Edwin H. Irvine, founder of Montana Collegiate Institute, 1878.

Deer Lodge campus, 1880s.

Chapter One
Seedtime in Deer Lodge

"The journey of a thousand miles starts with a single step."
— *Chinese proverb*

The second oldest town in Montana was also the first to start a school of higher learning. That might have been expected of Deer Lodge, fortunate in its location in a well-watered valley, where Indians had wintered with the whitetail deer and trappers had lived in temporary dwellings. Its wealth of natural resources had early attracted gold-seekers, cattlemen, merchants, brewers, and the first bankers in the territory. Travelers en route West on the Mullan Road helped fuel the economy with their purchases and repairs of broken wagon wheels. Miners passing through on their way to the gold camps found Deer Lodge to be a "good little town."[1] For Granville Stuart, pioneer stockman and prominent citizen, writing in 1876, Deer Lodge with its well laid out streets and handsome houses was easily "the most beautiful town in the territory, if not in the Rocky Mountains."[2]

He was also impressed with its patriotic and progressive citizenry, which at one time or another had included many of the territory's leaders. Another observer in the summer of 1869 described Deer Lodge as "peopled by a relatively larger number of families than other towns, and thus having an inherent social superiority."[3] That made for an early interest in education, with Deer Lodge County levying the first school taxes to be recorded in Montana. The first grade school building was a cramped, log affair in which, it was said, it would be "impossible to entertain a full-grown visitor, or even a liberal idea."[4] A larger replacement came in 1869, with the good ladies of Deer

Lodge giving a ball to raise funds for the completion of the building. Books were a common possession in town, with the Granville Stuarts claiming a library of 3,000 volumes.

So the time and the place seemed right when Edwin Irvine called a meeting in early 1878 to discuss the founding of a college. He intended a non-sectarian school, though one with a religious emphasis in its offerings. Men such as Conrad Kohrs, Edward Larabie, William Andrews Clark, and Judge Hiram Knowles voiced strong support and joined in an effort to raise money. *The New North-West* for February 1 reported that $7,000 had been subscribed towards a goal of $12,000, with calls soon to be made elsewhere in the county.

Aside from having a college at home for children and teacher training, Irvine and others saw its benefits for a recovering economy. *The New North-West* editorialized:

> It is the first practical note of revival in our town, and is the key to a harmony that will fill the air with revived industry and thrift ..... The institute will bring many families here for its educational advantages, but this is only one of the many advantages that will be derived from the new impetus and faith it has already given to the town.[5]

Such reassurances were needed with population trends beginning to favor Butte. That languishing gold camp roused with the discovery of silver and then of copper, which would send Butte on its way to becoming the largest city in the region.[6] Deer Lodge banker, Institute backer, and future copper king W.A. Clark would be among those moving to "the richest hill on earth."

On the 14th of February, the Deer Lodge County Teachers Institute passed a resolution in support of a school "in which shall be taught the useful and ornamental branches of education." Irvine was on hand, affirming that they were about to "found an institution of which Montana would be proud."[7] By March 8, the local press was reporting that sufficient funds had been raised in town, with promises from Butte, Philipsburg, and Pioneer to warrant a meeting to discuss organization and construction of a building.

Montana Collegiate Institute ▓

That meeting occurred on March 30 when subscribers to the "Collegiate Institute Fund" convened at the courthouse. Irvine was elected president of the founding body, with school superintendent Addison Smith serving as secretary. Judge Hiram Knowles briefed the meeting on incorporation procedures and a committee was appointed to follow through. Episcopal Rector Mahlon N. Gilbery moved the name of "Montana Collegiate Institute, " which was duly adopted. Trustees were elected and confirmed at a later meeting.

Territorial law (Town Site Act of Montana Territory) provided that towns could set aside 20 acres, to be held in trust by the probate judge for college purposes. The building committee, including Granville Stuart, was already eying the elevated plateau southwest of the Catholic church and hospital. It had once been a favorite spot for him to hunt whitetail deer. On May 31, 48 petitioners (only 20 were required by law) addressed Probate Judge O. B. O'Bannon with the appropriate document and the land was transferred to the Institute.

There was talk at first of having a building ready by fall, but there were delays and the contractor was given until late December to complete construction. Since school was to start in September, temporary quarters were needed and were found in a vacated Methodist church. A partition was added to the log structure to provide two rooms. Accommodations were rented elsewhere for the music program. Thus housed, President Clayton H. Moore with two colleagues and 30 plus students were ready to sow some seeds of higher learning in Montana. It was, indeed, as James Bryce would say, a humble beginning. Yet, it was a beginning and, as *The New North-West* noted, "Deer Lodgers are determined upon having the educational city of the Territory."[8] Some of its citizens would have even bolder visions, as they saw their town becoming the "Athens" of the North-West.

Moore was principal of the Deer Lodge School when he accepted the Institute's presidency at a salary of $1,800 for a ten months term. A native of New Hampshire, with a farm boy's upbringing, he had both A.B. and A.M. degrees from Dartmouth, and had taught in Vermont and Nevada before coming to Deer Lodge in 1877. Bozeman had hoped to attract him there and the *Avant Courier* for April 25, 1878 sent congratulations that the Institute had acquired one who "is said to be the best educator now in the Territory."

In June, Moore embarked on a trip back East to interview and hire two teachers and to purchase the needed "apparatus" for class-room work. With shallow pockets, he had the unenviable task of staffing and equipping a program which also had to include some grade-school preparation. A more exalted version of the Institute's mission found expression in *The New North-West* for April 26, 1878.

> Instruction will be given in all the branches taught in any Academy in the east, and students who desire will be fitted to enter Harvard or Yale direct. Teachers of public schools can take instructions in those branches relating to their work. Music, Painting, French, German and the Sciences will receive particular attention, and the President will endeavor to provide for the young ladies and gentlemen of Montana all the educational advantages they can secure in an institution of the same class in any of the States.

Moore's stay back East was productive, and on July 26, 1878 he wrote home from Milwaukee, Wisconsin that he had earlier shipped from Boston "the finest and most complete Philosophical apparatus owned between California and Kansas." A first-class piano and furniture for the classrooms were also on their way. He was especially pleased with his two assistant teachers, who would be leaving with him for Deer Lodge on August 5th. He would be forwarding shortly a prospectus for the Institute, which should be circulated widely to assure a good entering class.

Moore lacked one credential common to presidents of small west-ern colleges, especially with denominational ties, namely, ministerial status; otherwise, he shared the scattered responsibilities of that office. For his teaching assignment, he was to range over the Classics, Science, and Mathematics. Miss Grace G. Pike of Middleboro, Connecticut would handle French and German, having studied the languages abroad during a two years' residency. She had been teaching at an academy in Illinois for the past three years. Miss Anna N. King of Morristown, New Jersey would head the music program, with ten years teaching experience in Virginia, Florida, and other Atlantic Coast states.

Funding efforts for the Institute included a trip to Butte in August, with *The Weekly Miner* on the 27th reporting that Colonel L.J. Sharp and Mr. Ed. H. Irvine of Deer Lodge had returned home with "the very respectable sum of $2,400" contributed. They had missed visiting in Walkerville and with some of the town's "most liberal citizens" who were away, so Butte's final investment, the *Miner* was confident, would be over $4,000. For that matter, the paper declared, "it is the duty of every true Montanan to exert himself in (the Institute's) behalf." Facilities for learning were sorely needed beyond the free, graded schools, where sons and daughters could share in the privileges of their eastern cousins and benefit from the life of "a well cultivated mind." Further, the presence of educational facilities would attract the kind of settlers Montana needed.

President Moore's prospectus announced an academic year of three terms, beginning September 9, 1878. There were three courses of study, exclusive of the music program: College Preparatory, The Classical Graduating Course, and English and Business, designed for careers in commerce. Tuition varied from $15.00 to $18.75 per term, payable in advance, with additional fees for music lessons. An added attraction for female students was the opportunity to have room and board with the Institute's lady teachers, to share, as *The Weekly Miner* for October 1 observed, the cultural values of "refined companionship, and brilliant conversation of cultivated ladies."

Unfortunately, the first class of thirty plus contained few out-of-town students and none from Butte. That fact concerned the *Miner*, both in view of the town's financial contribution to the Institute and that the facilities now existed "for the education of girls....such as were never before offered in Montana. No parent need have any misgivings in entrusting his daughter to the Montana Collegiate Institute."[9] There were applications from elsewhere, but the lack of room and board facilities was a major hindrance to enrollment.

Deer Lodgers that fall and winter watched the work progress on what was billed to be the handsomest building in the territory. *The New North-West* on November 8 reported that the project was on schedule and found the two-story brick structure to be "solid, substantial, and enduring." That remark proved to be prophetic, for well over a century later, Trask Hall still stands and is used by the Deer Lodge Public Schools.

While the building was enclosed, it remained unfinished, due to cost overruns and the cancellation of some subscriptions. Much of the equipment purchased by Moore remained boxed awaiting space for its use, though Miss King did have available the new Weber's Grand Piano. While there was some sagging of spirits among Institute enthusiasts, ladies in town rallied with a week-long fair in April to benefit the school. Ella (Irvine) Mountjoy later recalled:

> They canvassed the town and country around for donations of food and also fancy work and any articles of artistic or useful value. They held the fair for one week serving lunch and dinner. They held raffles and games and lotteries, and contests, and cleared $1500. They were elated over their success and decided to hold another fair in the fall. At this one they cleared $1800.[10]

Thanks largely to such efforts, the building was finally completed in December of 1880. For Deer Lodgers who had bought into the dream, there was cause for rejoicing at a ball and housewarming held in the new hall on December 27, 1880. It was cold in the valley, but it was warm inside as happy celebrants made the most of the occasion. For years to come, the building on the slope just east of downtown would symbolize the yearnings for a better way of life found in an educated citizenry.

The first and only year for the Institute had its ups and downs. Ella remembered that for the students it was a good and memorable one. They had profited from excellent instruction and by April, during examination week, were able to impress a visiting committee of trustees with their accomplishments. *The New North-West* applauded their performances on April 11, 1879:

> That the first year of the Institute, now drawing to a close, has been a successful one, no one who has attended the examinations made of the studies gone over during the past year can deny. If before there was any room for doubt, this doubt has been dispelled by the manifest proficiency of the pupils in their various studies.

Through its talented faculty of three, the Institute that year also had a beneficial presence in community life and beyond. Anna King and Grace Pike were in constant demand for concert appearances, along with the student chorus. Their efforts at a performance in early December, 1878, won high praise from the press. "It was unexceptionally the finest entertainment ever given in the town, and received, as it merited, the highest encomiums from all."[11] Over in Butte, William A. Clark took notice of such talent and scheduled appearances there.

By April, 1879, Edwin Irvine had to be worried about finances. Enrollment had been discouragingly low, minimizing tuition income upon which the trustees had depended. Some subscriptions had been canceled. Irvine personally had incurred considerable indebtedness on behalf of the school. His report to the stockholders may also have implied some disappointment with leadership.* Yet, he remained forward-looking:

> If in your future election of managers you will select men who will directly cooperate together, and without a doubt or hesitation work faithfully and confidently together, you will see erected on these foundations so well laid an institution which will be to the future State of Montana what the great colleges and seminaries of Europe have been to her, and what Yale and Harvard, the Universities of Virginia and Missouri and all the other innumerable institutions of the United States have been and are to her....See to it that in your selection of trustees for the ensuing year you select those who, regardless of religious, political or party bias, will foster it, care for it and protect it from all harm.[12]

In addition to Irvine, the new board included prominent men such as Conrad Kohrs, O.B. O'Bannon, W.A. Clark, and Granville Stuart. But when the third term ended in late June 1879, it was decided not to open in the fall. Resources were exhausted, main supporters overly committed, while the unfinished building on the hillside seemed to mock the high hopes of the year before. The corporation of stockholders, however, remained in place with its board of trustees, to keep alive possibilities for beginning again. Such an eventuality was clear for Irvine, even if he had to operate a school largely on his own. Perhaps a metaphor for that first year was something like a false dawn, such as sailors sometimes see, that precedes the real dawn.

* Sources do not clearly differentiate between "trustees" and "stockholders," nor do they clearly indicate either for-profit or non-profit status for the institution. Some governance issues remain unclear.

Deer Lodgers were not prepared to concede that the sun would not yet rise and shine on the educational town in Montana Territory.

As for that intrepid first faculty, Clayton Moore took a teaching position in Boise, followed by a return to Montana and a postmastership in the new town of Anaconda. Anna King went abroad with the Conrad Kohrs family to study voice in Germany and then came back to Deer Lodge in the fall of 1882. The Presbyterians would invite her to join the faculty of their school. Grace Pike said good-bye to a large number of friends in town, accompanied Anna to Helena for a final concert there, and then took the river route home to Connecticut.

MOUNTJOY INTERLUDE

Though no school was in session that fall of 1879, women in Deer Lodge, as has been mentioned, held another successful fair, determined to see the Institute building completed. Progress from that point was noted, while trustees remained attentive to the possibilities of resuming instruction. Help came from an unexpected quarter, when the new Disciples minister in town approached them about leasing Institute equipment and a part of the new building when it became available.

Reverend Wiley Mountjoy was from a Missouri Disciples family, a recent graduate of Christian University at Canton, Missouri, who accepted the post of organizing pastor of the Christian Church in Deer Lodge. Arriving in July of 1880, he soon took notice of the building east of town. Ambitious and energetic, disposed towards teaching as well as preaching, he negotiated successfully with the trustees. *The New North-West* for August 13 reported:

> Having made arrangement with the Trustees of the Montana Collegiate Institute, Mr. W. Mountjoy will open a private school in the college building on Monday, Sept. 13th. Mr. Mountjoy is a thorough graduate, a teacher of experience and comes highly recommended. The Institute is a need in Montana, and residents of this county particularly should interest themselves in seeing it is made a success. A large amount of money has been expended in the erection of the building and in the purchase of apparatus, etc. We are glad to know that a school will be started, and trust ere long the attendance will be large enough to warrant the securing of additional teachers.

Mountjoy advertised an academic year with two terms of sixteen weeks each. Tuition for the collegiate department would be $30, and $20 for preparatory work. He aimed to provide instruction in the higher education branches, including Latin and Greek. School opened again in the vacated Methodist church, with a subsequent move to the new building. In later years, Mountjoy remembered that he had about twenty-five students, some of whom "had attended the College of Prof. Moore." He did not dignify his endeavor "by New Name of College."[13]

Toward the end of the first year, Mountjoy renewed his request for use of the Institute building and classroom equipment. He committed to finding a music teacher, to a canvass of the territory in the upcoming summer to recruit students, and to hold himself responsible for any damage to the building or apparatus. The lease was renewed, and by July of 1881 he had hired Miss L. Carrie Grimes of Camden Point, Missouri to handle the music assignment. Like Anna King, she, too, proved efficient, attracting enough students to require an additional piano and opening a singing school for interested townspeople. After a year, she returned to Missouri, where she died shortly of pneumonia at the young age of nineteen.

Mountjoy also added a second teacher. Meanwhile, a bond grew with one of his students, and in the summer of 1882 he married Ella Irvine. His brother John traveled from Missouri to officiate at the union. The new Mrs. Mountjoy also felt the urge to teach, and the couple decided to leave Deer Lodge to take the superintendency of the Camden Point Female Academy in Missouri.[14]

Presbyterian Involvement

Earlier that year the Institute stockholders and board had reviewed the school's chances for success and concluded that a facility for room and board would have to be added to accommodate out-of-town students. Otherwise, there would be no growth in enrollment. The local press agreed in that assessment: "The inability to procure these (students) has been the great detriment from the first. The past winter there were dozens of applications made and boarding facilities could not be had."[15] The time was at hand to find some person or group capable of building a dormitory and meeting other needs of an expanded student body.

That prompted a meeting of the stockholders on Friday evening, February 17 at Judge O.B. O'Bannon's office. Edwin H. Irvine presided and reviewed the existing situation. The Collegiate Institute was $5,000 in debt, most of it owed to the Donnell, Clark & Larabie Bank. Assets estimated at $20,000 consisted of the school building, "instruments and apparatus, " six blocks on "College Hill" and about $3,000 of unpaid and uncollectable subscriptions.

Irvine came prepared with a solution and an invitation for nineteen supporters to join him in liquidating the remaining debt. Furthermore, he would assume responsibility for operating a nonsectarian school for ten years, including the building of a dormitory. At the end of the period, he would either purchase or return the school property to the stockholders. If given time, he would provide further details at a later meeting.

That happened on the 25th at Fireman's Hall, where the Institute stalwart agreed to assume indebtedness of not over $5,000. Additionally, he would have a dormitory in place for teachers and students by September 10, 1882. He would recruit a competent faculty to handle a curriculum including English, Mathematics, Sciences, Languages, and Music. The school's orientation would be nonpartisan and nonsectarian. The trustees, he proposed, should sell two blocks of land, with proceeds applied to ridding the campus of sage brush and cactus and otherwise improving the grounds. The stockholders approved his plan and authorized the trustees to move ahead.

There was another proposal, however, at the February 17th meeting brought by Reverend James R. Russel, former Presbyterian pastor in town, now located in Butte but still interested in Institute affairs. More than that, he represented his denomination's commitment to education on the frontier. It was viewed as an essential part of Christian missions. The General Assembly had established in 1877 a committee to study enlarging the responsibilities of the Board of Education to fund colleges and seminaries. That committee found a definite need for more colleges in the West, and reasoned that the Presbyterians not only needed a presence there but had a service to perform for the country.[16]

Earlier, in 1872, Presbyterians had established in Bozeman an academy for girls, which became the Gallatin Valley Female Seminary. That work had gone well under the leadership of Reverend Lyman B. Crittenden and his wife and had earned the praise of the Montana Presbytery at its meeting in Helena in February, 1876. By the session on August 12, 1881, the Presbytery was actively pursuing possibilities for an institution of higher learning, assigning Russel and Reverend Robert H. Howey to investigate a location in Helena. It was to be called Montana University. Later, the local pastor, Reverend William B. Reed, was charged with raising money for the school. Very little happened in that regard.

Meanwhile, events in Deer Lodge were of particular concern to Russel, and he came to the February 17th gathering with a bid, not yet authorized by the Presbytery. He proposed that the bank continue to hold the debt at an 8% interest for the next ten years, while the Presbyterians had use of the campus to conduct a "good school." At the end, they would retire all indebtedness, either continuing operations or returning the facilities to the stockholders. He was back in town in April promoting his solution, noting that the Presbytery would be meeting in August, when he felt assured of a favorable response.

The denomination's Board of Home Missions had added Montana and Idaho to the Utah district. It was noted that Montana people "were enterprising and intelligent pioneers, " with "doctors and lawyers, men and women interested in music and other arts as well as those whose chief concern was with the mines." The territory had excellent schools and "teachers of a high order." But an institution of higher learning was needed, especially one affiliated with the Presbyterian Church. For that denomination "has special affinities for learning and everywhere it has done a lasting work in planting schools, academies and colleges."[17]

Sentiment among trustees and stockholders shifted in support of transferring the school to the Presbytery, with the influential Judge Hiram Knowles voicing his support for such a course of action. *The New North-West* sought to reassure those who wanted a nonsectarian institution.

In thus deviating from the original intent of establishing and maintaining a strictly non-sectarian school, the Trustees had done what was deemed the best that could be done in carrying out the wishes and intent of the stockholders in the Institute, viz., to secure the establishment and maintenance of an Institute of Learning under the direction of an organization having the will and the means to successfully conduct it.[18]

As Russel had predicted, the Montana Presbytery, at its Helena meeting on August 19, 1882, approved the purchase of the Deer Lodge school. The following resolution was adopted: "Resolved, that the Presbytery authorize the Rev. Messrs. D.J. McMillan, E.J. Groeneveld, and J.R. Russel, to negotiate for and, if expedient, buy the Montana Collegiate Institute, in Deer Lodge, for the Presbytery of Montana."[19] Fortuitously, Groeneveld had met one William Allanson Trask of Brooklyn, New York, who was passing through the territory. Trask was the legatee of a sizable estate and became interested in the Deer Lodge venture, proceeding to pay off the entire indebtedness. Thus the property was conveyed to the Presbytery free of obligation. For his generosity, the building on "College Hill" was named for him. His benefactions would continue through the years.

The new Board of Trustees, appointed by the Presbytery, consisted of Reverends James R. Russel, Eiko J. Groeneveld, Duncan J. McMillan (Missionary Superintendent from Salt Lake City), John T. Forbis, prominent attorney, and Samuel T. Hauser, capitalist, Helena banker, and later (briefly) territorial governor. It fell to Forbis, who was serving in the legislature, to introduce a bill providing for the incorporation of educational institutions. A law was enacted and the new school was incorporated in March of 1884 adopting the name "The College of Montana" — fortunately abandoning the more pretentious "Montana University."

The articles of incorporation placed the college under "the auspices of the Presbyterian Church in the United States" and provided that the "particular character of the institution shall be that of a college for the instruction of young men and women in literature, in arts, in the sciences, and all branches of learning, that may be embraced in and requisite for a liberal education."[20] Russel and colleagues hoped to open with classes in September, 1882, but the time was far too short for recruitment of faculty and students. So they settled for beginning the next fall.

For Deer Lodgers, the building east of town took on an added significance with a fresh envisagement of their community as a center of learning. Talk of a "university town," even an "Athens of the West" would reach as far as Salt Lake, with the local press there taking note of developments in Montana. It was a time to be savored, of hopes and enthusiasms kindled anew. Duncan McMillan caught the spirit and agreed to serve as the fledgling institution's first president.

Dr. Duncan J. McMillan, first president of the College of Montana, 1883–1890.

Hon. Cornelius Hedges, Montana Superintendent of Public Instruction and supporter of the College of Montana.

Rev. Eiko Groeneveld, D.D., founder and faculty member of the College of Montana

Steel engraving by M.J. Conn

Conrad Kohrs, pioneer stockman and supporter of the Institute.

Faculty of the College of Montana, 1887 Prof. Frank M. Notestein, Miss Mary B. Hill, Prof. F.D. Kelsey, Miss Lizzie Woolfolk, Miss Lena Vaughn, Prof. Theodore Brantly, Miss Lois Reat, Miss Kate Calvin, Prof. Frank Traphagen and Pres. Duncan McMillan, D.D.

Chapter Two
College of Montana

"In some of these smaller Western colleges one finds to-day men of great ability and great attainment, one finds students who are receiving an education as thorough, though not always as wide as the best Eastern universities can give."
— *James Bryce*

The founders had to be men of faith and vision, certain of the value of higher learning, for that year, 1882, the Presbytery of Montana consisted of seven ministers, ten churches, 295 members, with total congregational expenditures of $6,275. The entire territorial population of around 40,000, scattered over the distances, would hardly make a good-sized town back East. It was, to be sure, the onset of rapid growth in the region, with the coming of the railroads, developments in agriculture, and the boom in mining. By 1892, there were 26 clergy, 25 churches, 2,307 members and $44,751 in congregational support. Membership would double by the turn of the century.[1]

THE FIRST PRESIDENT

Reverend Duncan James McMillan was not unacquainted with challenges. A native of Tennessee, he had come West from Illinois to minister around Salt Lake City. Known as an "above average preacher, " he was chosen in 1880 to serve as Presbyterian Mission Superintendent for Utah and Montana. Idaho was added later. That was part of the geography that had been assigned in 1869 to the indefatigable Sheldon Jackson as Missionary Superintendent for the Western Territories, reflecting the woeful ignorance of Eastern mission boards of the vastness of the regions to be served. Jackson extended Presbyterian missions into Alaska and went there as Superintendent in 1884. He had set a hectic pace for the new man.

McMillan found territory enough to keep him "on the wing." He later remembered the ardors of travel, particularly in the sub zero weather, when "sleighing, staging, or private conveyance were the only possible means of travel. The times were strenuous, snows deep, winters cold, and prices high."[2] The Montana frontier, however, held pleasant surprises. Thus, in the silver camp of Granite, conducting worship "in an upper room of a rude board building, " he found six college graduates in the congregation, including one from Yale and another from Union College. That mattered to him, and along with the kind and considerate ways of frontier people, compensated for the trying times, as when he got lost in a mountain pass on his way to Fort Benton.

That happened on his first visit to Montana in January, 1881. He arrived by rail at Dillon, just a few days after the Utah and Northern had reached that tent and shanty town on its way to Butte and the lucrative mining trade. The place proudly bore the name of the railroad's president, Sidney Dillon. Unfortunately, there was little reason for McMillan to linger; the Methodists were already there. A Presbyterian church would be formed late in the decade. Glendale was equally disappointing, for this time Baptists outnumbered other faiths. Gracious in spirit, the mission superintendent offered to find for them "a good deep water Baptist" preacher.

Those and other visits were seasoning experiences for the man who would assume the college presidency in Deer Lodge. Shortly after that happened, in August of 1882, he was on his way East, looking for financial support. By then the Northern Pacific had reached in, providing relative comfort in travel. Again, he was among the early passengers to take advantage of this new mode of transportation. His primary destination was the New York and Brooklyn area, where Adamson Trask could provide an "in" with potential donors.

McMillan's initial efforts produced about $10,000, including Trask's commitment to cover the president's salary for the next three years. That amounted to $2,000 annually, prompting him to write home that he would be able "to lay by a good deal every year." He would also continue with his mission post until December 1885. *The New North-West* for July 20, 1883 noted that the college "desired to raise $40,000 to $50,000," so there was considerable work to be done.

EARLY YEARS 🪷

The new school opened its doors on September 10, 1883. Villagers heard the bell on "college hill" ring promptly at 8:30 A.M., announcing the renewal of higher learning in Montana Territory. Few doubted that this was where it belonged, in their peaceful, scenic valley, rimmed by the main range of the Rockies to the East, with majestic Mt. Powell to the West, towering to 10,500 feet. Free from the distractions of mining towns and commercial centers, Deer Lodge was a community of moral tone equal to the best anywhere. So the local citizenry reasoned, as they also were confident that this day marked only a beginning. A spacious campus of 20 acres, overlooking Main Street and valley, had plenty of room for the growth that would surely occur.

Deer Lodge promoters of the college, including the local press, had preferred a nonsectarian institution, but were reassured by an announcement in *The New North-West* for August 3, 1883:

> While this school is under the auspices of the Presbyterian Board of Education, Mr. McMillan informs us it is not, as might be supposed, denominational in its character. No creed or dogma is taught in the school, no restraint placed on the free will of the pupils as to their church attendance or affiliations, and one teacher at least, now engaged, and perhaps a majority of the teachers and trustees will be members of other churches than the Presbyterian.

A faculty of five had been recruited to range over a curriculum featuring a Normal Course for those preparing to teach, a Scientific Course designed to equip students for the "occupations in these mountain states and territories, " and a Classical Course "which is the usual curriculum of college studies."[3]

In addition to his presidential duties, McMillan would handle both the Natural Sciences and Ancient Languages. That fall brought an honorary Doctor of Divinity degree from Washington and Jefferson College in Pennsylvania, which was met with hearty approval among colleagues, students, and friends in the community.

Joining him on the faculty was Prof. Arthur M. Mattoon, A.M. from Albany, Oregon and the Collegiate Institute there, teaching Mathematics and English. His wife assisted with English and served as Matron for boarding students. Rev. Eiko J. Groeneveld, A.M. taught part time German and English Literature. A Princeton graduate, he had taken the Presbyterian church in town and was a mover behind the new college. Miss Nellie A. Hutchinson of New Albany, Indiana instructed in vocal and instrumental music. Groeneveld also served on the governing board, along with McMillan, Presbyterian pastor James Russel of Butte, Hon. John F. Forbis of Butte, and Helena capitalist Samuel T. Hauser.

The first *Annual Catalogue* (1883-84) reported a student body of 47, "25 ladies and 22 gentlemen." The *Normal Course* led with an enrollment of 18, followed closely by music studies with 16. Most came from Deer Lodge and neighboring communities, though several had home addresses in Connecticut, New York, and Tennessee. Trask Hall was ready on that September morning, providing a refectory in the ample basement, with study and recitation rooms on the first and second floors. In addition, the large "anniversary hall" and two study rooms provided temporary housing quarters. To aid instruction, "all necessary philosophical and chemical apparatus" had been purchased, along with two pianos and an organ.

The energetic president had little time to spare as he divided responsibilities with fund raising and the classroom. Some support came from the denomination, from the Presbyterian Board of Aid for Colleges and Academies created by the General Assembly in 1883. Its first report for 1884 indicated that $29,000 had been divided among nine institutions, with the greater part distributed to four of them. The College of Montana at Deer Lodge was one of the four. Further, it was among the Presbyterian-related schools to receive support through the decade.[4]

Additionally, the Board was helpful in providing authorization for calls upon Presbyterian donors in the New York—Brooklyn area. A document dated June 6th, 1884 declared that:

> This certifies that the Presbyterian Board of Aid for Colleges and Academies has assigned to the Presbyterian College located at Deer Lodge, Montana, as the special field in which to solicit gifts for buildings and endowment, the Cities of New York

and Brooklyn. The Board of Aid, being acquainted with the character and needs of this institution, intends this assignment of territory as its most formal commendation of the Presbyterian College at Deer Lodge to the confidence and liberality of Presbyterian givers.[5]

> *H.D. Ganse*
> *Sec. B.A.C.A.*

President McMillan was encouraged with developments. In early March, 1884, he wrote to his mother:

> This is truly a busy world & it seems to grow busier & busier. Well, "The College of Montana" — the name by which we have incorporated — is a fixed fact. We have very flattering prospects - but we *must have* enlarged accommodations. So I go East very soon, about April 1st, to raise money for the purpose of enlarging the buildings. I go so early in order to raise money before rich people go off for vacation.

Later that month, he wrote again:

> I am on my way home to Salt Lake to spend a few days with my family and then start East...I am very much pleased with my College work. This—the first year— is far more prosperous than we anticipated. We have an excellent class of patronage. We are waiting and working with great encouragement. Our prospects are brightening all the time and the demands are for enlarged accommodations. We want dormitories for both sexes and must have them if we grow. One man in Deer Lodge offers $1000 toward a dormitory building. With that offer as a starter I hope to accomplish the task this spring.[6]

It would be another year before a dormitory was constructed. Meanwhile, McMillan could view accomplishments to date with evident satisfaction. He wrote in the first *Catalogue*:

> The College of Montana has no apology to offer for its existence. It was determined by that hunger for higher education which an excellent public school system creates. It came into being in response to a call from all parts of a vast region of country into which population is flowing. It is without a rival within a circle whose radius is five hundred miles. It is closing its first year with results which surpass the most hopeful anticipations. And greater things than these would have been realized had our boarding accommodations been more extensive.

Housing needs were first met with the building of a dormitory in 1885. It contained quarters for 70 students, plus kitchen and dining facilities, and a reading room. The *Catalogue* for that year noted: "This building is under the supervision of a Matron of wisdom and experience, who also has the personal oversight of each student boarding in the College. She is assisted by several members of the Faculty, who occupy rooms in the dormitory." Evidently, little was left undone in the fulfillment of the school's responsibilities of *in loco parentis*. The addition of a second building was designated the "Ladies Dormitory."

As anticipated, expanded housing facilities resulted in larger enrollments — 80 in 1885, 130 in 1888, 160 by 1890. Other factors feeding growth included an enlarged curriculum, a more specialized faculty, and a widening reputation for excellence. The 1888-89 Academic Year featured in addition to the Classical, Scientific and Normal Courses a School of Mines, a Conservatory of Music, and an Academy for college preparation.

Mining and smelting had become the leading industries in Montana. In copper production, Butte operators (mainly Anaconda) were competing successfully with the Lake Superior Mines. "Copper King" William Andrews Clark and others determined that instruction in mining, engineering and metallurgy should be available in the region, specifically, at the College of Montana. He led off with a substantial contribution to purchase equipment and to bring Augustus M. Ryan, A.M., and Frank W. Traphagen, Ph.D., to Deer Lodge. Both were graduates from Columbia University School of Mines. The latter came in 1887 to teach Chemistry and Metallurgy, while Ryan arrived the following year to organize a department of mining engineering. They would remain in Deer Lodge until 1893, when they joined the new state school in Bozeman.

Another venture in professional training would come in 1895 with the introduction of a School of Pharmacy. The State Legislature had passed a more stringent law regulating the practice of Pharmacy, making formal study more of a necessity. Since there were no schools within a thousand miles of Montana, Deer Lodge trustees authorized the establishment of a program and the employment of a Chemist-Pharmacist. Fortunately, some of the laboratory equipment which William Andrews Clark had purchased for mining also proved to be useful.

Meanwhile, the Conservatory continued to play an important role in the life of the college, combining both the Departments of Music and Fine Arts. It enrolled more students than any other area. In fact, in 1888, more than one half of the college registrations were in the Conservatory. Fine Arts instruction included oil and water colors, portrait and china painting, free hand and charcoal drawing, modeling and wood carving. The *Catalogue* for that year observed that the "location of the College is highly favorable to the cultivation of the artist. Clear atmosphere, pure air, mountain grandeur and landscape beauty inspire and sustain his activities" (p. 38).

For students generally, elocution and voice culture classes were a requirement, as proper preparation for social and professional life. In matters of refinement, it was the school's intention that parents needed to look no further than what was available in Deer Lodge. Two literary societies provided further exposure to cultural taste and expression, namely, "The Gamma Theta" and "The Philo Kalian." The latter was restricted to the lady students. Both the Y.M.C.A. and Y.W.C.A. had active programs on the campus. Thanks to generous donors, including several from back East, the library holdings were growing and the Reading Room was stocked with regional newspapers and magazines. Daily chapel was a reminder of the school's religious orientation.

The benefits of physical exercise were not neglected, with a women's gymnasium occupying part of the basement in new North Hall. A high ceiling allowed for playing the new game of basketball, along with other sports. By the late 1880s, there was talk of adding a gymnasium to the college plant. The campus contained baseball and football fields, tennis courts, and a large skating rink, a favorite place to congregate on winter evenings.

By the late 1880s, the faculty numbered fifteen members spread over the several departments. There was a sprinkling of graduate degrees from leading universities. James J. Robinson, in Latin and Greek, was a product of Princeton University. Irving Babbitt, in Modern Languages, was from Harvard. Theodore S. Brantly, in Mining Law, had studies at Southwestern University. Frank M. Notestein held the A.M. from Wooster University and taught Mathematics and Astronomy. As noted earlier, Augustus Ryan and Frank W. Traphagen had studied at Columbia University School of Mines.

Of those who taught in Deer Lodge during the "great days" of the late 1880s and early 1890s, none was destined for more acclaim than young Irving Babbitt. Born in Dayton, Ohio in 1865, the promising Harvard scholar spent two years (1889–1891) at the College of Montana, before leaving to continue studies at the Sorbonne, thence to return to Cambridge in 1894 as professor of French Literature. There he would pursue an illustrious career until his death in 1933. Babbitt was the leading proponent for the movement called "New Humanism," seeking to correct the excesses of the romanticists in modern thought and art by a return to classical traditions.

James M. Self, the first college librarian, later became a distinguished Montana jurist, while Theodore Brantly would serve from 1899 to 1921 as Chief Justice of the State Supreme Court. Augustus Ryan became the first president of the Montana State College in Bozeman. These people and others remind one of James Bryce's comment. In his classic, *The American Commonwealth*, the visiting English historian and statesman observed: "In some of these smaller Western colleges one finds to-day men of great ability and great attainment, one finds students who are receiving an education as thorough, though not always as wide as the best Eastern universities can give."[7]

Along with an able faculty, the College of Montana also benefited from the guidance and support of a governing board that included prominent Montanans. Among them were: Governor Samuel T. Hauser, Judge Decius Wade, S.E. Larabie, Conrad Kohrs, Cornelius Hedges, John F. Forbis, and William Andrews Clark. Hedges' contribution came from a distinguished career as Superintendent of Public Instruction. A product of both Yale and Harvard, the New Englander infused frontier schooling with the importance of an educated citizenry. He well deserved the designation "founder of the Montana territorial school system." He was no passive onlooker at events in Deer Lodge.

McMillan was well positioned to travel in search of funds. Deer Lodge was on the Utah and Northern, near its junction with the Northern Pacific, facilitating visits in several directions. Adamson Trask remained the major benefactor, with gifts totaling over $20,000. Next in line was W.H. Murray of Chicago, followed by Montanans S.E. Larabie, E.L. Bonner, Edwin H. Irvine, and Conrad Kohrs. As noted earlier, William A. Clark invested in the School of Mines.

Tiring of too many appeals, Trask tightened the purse strings in the spring of 1887, pending more support from the region. It was not the best of times to do so, for the severe winter of 1886-87, "The Great White Death," had left the cattle industry decimated. McMillan faced an indebtedness that July of nearly $6,000 and wrote to college trustee Samuel T. Hauser outlining the situation, suggesting further contact with Board president Clark, Kohrs, Larabie, and Bonner. "Old Man Trask," he reported, "will not give another dollar till Montana does more. Then he will about duplicate what we do I think. Let me hear from you with any suggestions you may have to offer."[8]

McMillan wrote to Hauser again on October 19th, reporting further developments:

> I have raised $10,000 upon condition that we raise $15,000 more in Montana. This $10,000 is offered by a Montana man who doesn't want his name made known until the whole $25,000 is raised. I want very much to see you a few minutes. Can I see you next Tuesday 25th. If not — when? I am *confident* that if we raise the $25,000 in Montana, old man Trask will duplicate it. Otherwise, he won't give us a cent more.

As the territory's leading capitalist, Hauser was a key player. The native Kentuckian had come to Montana in 1862, prospected for a while, and then started banking. The first bank, in Virginia City in 1865, was followed by one in Helena the next year, then Butte, Fort Benton, and Missoula. He also had mining interests and was involved in the organization and construction of six branch railroads. President Grover Cleveland appointed him Territorial Governor in July, 1885 and he served for 18 months. Hauser was interested in education and would subscribe $5,000 to the new Methodist college in Helena.

Along with the ever-present concern for operating funds, there was the need for endowments. An interesting addition to the 1885–86 *Catalogue* featured an explanation for such giving.

> It is a well known fact that no college can live and grow without income from other sources than the tuition of students. To demand from students the payment of an amount sufficient to support the Faculty of the college would eventually close the institution or at least forever bar from its privileges all that class which furnishes many of our leading men and ripest scholars......Endowment funds must always be provided. (p.22)

Ministers in the Montana Presbytery had set a "noble example," with gifts "wrung from their slender salaries" to endow a scholarship. The college, the *Catalogue* continued, was located in a

...territory with its rapidly accumulating wealth from mine and pasture and field and forest, and with its multiplying private fortunes. It is hoped that the College of Montana will soon find friends who will endow and equip it for influence and accomplishment worthy of the great field in the midst of which it is planted. (p. 22).

Though Duncan McMillan struggled with finances, it was his good fortune to preside during the school's most productive years. The College of Montana had a respectable faculty, a good enrollment, and a campus of 20 acres with four buildings valued at $100,000. It had acquired in the territory a solid reputation for learning. The president felt free enough of college responsibilities to run for a seat in the new State Senate. On October 1, 1889, Montanans approved overwhelmingly the proposed Constitution and, in a spirited election, voted for their first legislature. McMillan was on the Republican ticket in Deer Lodge County and lost to his Democrat opponent by about 300 votes. His defeat doubtless figured in his determination that the time had come to move on. That happened with his acceptance of a position with the Presbyterian Home Missionary Board in New York.

His resignation brought expressions of appreciation from several quarters. William A. Clark wrote from New York on March 25, 1890:

Dear Sir: — I must congratulate you upon the success of your earnest efforts in the direction of securing the greatest possible success for the College of Montana. The patrons of that Institution, and the citizens of Deer Lodge as well as the State at large, are deeply indebted to you for the interest you have manifested in the welfare of that Institution, and the great success of it which is due in great measure to your personal zeal and influence. I understand you are going to take up your residence in New York, and if so I shall be glad to see you during my visits there.[9]

On May 13, 1890, McMillan also heard from Hervey D. Ganse, Secretary of the Presbyterian Board of Aid, in regard to the conditions for a $10,000 grant. The letter concluded: "With congratulations to you, to the college and to ourselves that your regime ends so happily."[10] The

College's first president would have enduring memories of his time in the West, the testings and occasional triumphs of a pioneer preacher and educator, working at the foundations upon which others would build.

TROUBLED DECADE

Reverend James Reid followed in the Deer Lodge presidency. A graduate of McGill University in Montreal, he was highly regarded for his sound scholarship and attractive personality. The school's future seemed bright with the promise of continued growth. Montana had finally achieved statehood, the population had more than tripled during the 1880s, the economy was robust with millionaires multiplying in places like Helena and Butte. They had their own social clubs and wintered in the South. Along with other communions, Presbyterianism was prospering, now with three Presbyteries, 40 ministers, 45 churches, and 2,816 members.[11] The Methodists had just opened a college in Helena, but there was ample room, it seemed, for both institutions in the vast intermountain region. The college in 1893 shared in the World's Columbian Exposition, sending an exhibit and a professor to Chicago, to the "White City" on the shore of Lake Michigan. The Deer Lodge school was among exhibitors from 72 countries who, from May through November, drew 27 million visitors from around the world. The Great Discoverer of 400 years earlier would have marveled at the dramatic uses of electricity for illumination and power.

But that year also produced developments that dimmed the prospects for both Presbyterian and Methodist institutions. First, financial panic gripped the country due to complicated causes: concern over the nation's declining gold supply, seen as validating the currency, repeal of the Sherman Silver Purchase Act providing for a bimetallist monetary policy and angering the mining West, collapse of foreign markets due to business distresses in Europe and elsewhere, several railroads passing into receivership, banks everywhere calling in loans, the ranks of the unemployed swelling around the land. In Montana, the silver issue was particularly explosive, with mining towns emptying almost overnight. Recovery would come slowly across the state and nation.

Enrollments dropped at both colleges. In fact, when Montana Wesleyan opened in the fall of 1893, there were only seven students at the welcoming assembly, outnumbered by the faculty on the platform. The future was further clouded for the private schools when, that same year, the Montana legislature launched the public university system. Paris Gibson wanted one institution in his town, Great Falls, and offered land and a cash endowment as incentives. The lawmakers, however, heeding pressures from several towns, opted for a multi-unit system, with a university in Missoula, an agriculture college in Bozeman, a school of mines in Butte, and a normal college in Dillon.

The result was a loss of both faculty and students to the public institutions. Augustus Ryan left the mining program in Deer Lodge to serve as the first president (1893–1897) at the college in Bozeman. He was followed there by James Reid, from 1897 to 1904. Other faculty and staff found more security and greater financial rewards in moving to the public institutions, where students could also attend at less cost. The problem for the private, church-related schools was noted by James Bryce:

> Not the least interesting of the phenomena of today is the struggle which goes on in the Middle and Western States between the greater, and especially the State universities, and the small denominational colleges. The latter, which used to have the field to themselves, are now afraid of being driven off it by the growth of the former, and are redoubling their exertions not only to increase their own resources and students but—at least in some States—to prevent the State university from obtaining larger grants from the State treasury. They allege that the unsectarian character of the State establishments, as well as the freedom allowed to their students, makes them less capable of giving a moral and religious training. But as the graduates of the State universities become numerous in the legislatures and influential generally, and as it is more and more clearly seen that the small colleges cannot, for want of funds, provide the various appliances — libraries, museums, laboratories, and so forth — which universities need, the balance seems likely to incline in favor of the State Universities.[12]

Bryce predicted that many of the small denominational colleges would become "places of preparatory training." That proved to be unduly pessimistic, though Deer Lodge would be among those which had to close completely. Two more presidents served out the troubled decade, Reverend George F. Danforth, 1894–95 and Reverend Albert B. Martin, 1895–1900. While all indebtedness had been removed, the college had little endowment, patronage was declining, and more students were going elsewhere. Actually, the last year of 1899–1900 the school was operated as a Young Ladies' Seminary, but that did not avert closure as the new century came.

Trustees hoped that it might be temporary, that the attractive campus would interest investors intent upon preserving Protestant, church-related higher education in the region. Historian George Edwards noted: "Efforts are now being made to that end, and it is hoped that they will succeed. There are many reasons why a Christian college in Montana should live and prosper. The Christian college originally set the standard of American education and has maintained it ever since."[13]

Meanwhile, the ferment for learning at Deer Lodge helped to leaven the quality of life in Montana and elsewhere. Many of the students graduated with honors and distinguished themselves in professional and business activities. A number of the administrators and teachers became leaders in education in the state and beyond. If the "Athens of the West" was not destined to be, its legacy was not to be ignored. And the years would bring another glimmer of hope, before the bell finally tolled on higher education in the town where it first had been heard.

Lewis T. Eaton   *Ernest T. Eaton*

Exercise and active participation in athletic sports was expected of all the students at the College of Montana. Above is the 1905 basketball team.

Chapter Three Montana College

"For with slight efforts, how should one obtain great results? It is foolish even to desire it."
— *Euripides*

The renewal of activity on the Deer Lodge campus came from an unexpected quarter. Two years had passed without any investors, when Ernest T. Eaton came from Iowa as a young school superintendent to the town of 1,500. His roots were in central Maine, younger son in a farm family that managed a living off the rock-strewn hillsides. Along with tutelage to the soil went a desire for education. Brother Lewis, older by eight years, peddled wild-berries to buy books and pay tuition at the academy three miles away. One took them for granted, the academies and colleges scattered throughout New England, keys to the future for many a determined youth. They belonged in a way of life that mattered to the Eaton family.

The Eatons became part of the westward surge in the post-Civil War years, relocating in eastern Iowa during the winter of 1886–87. Father Thomas O. Eaton and wife Delia Eaton settled at Earlville just west of Dubuque, where he opened a butchering business. Times were tough feeding a family of five, including daughter Alice. Later, another son, Volney, died in childhood. Lewis, at age 18, taught in a rural school and contributed his $30 a month to the family's livelihood. Following schooling at Northern Illinois Normal School and Highland Park College in Des Moines, he served as principal of schools at Earlville.

Meanwhile, Ernest had entered Lenox College, a Presbyterian school at Hopkington, Iowa. Following graduation, he taught for one year, studied further at the University of Iowa, served as a school principal in Des Moines and then as one of the state's youngest superintendents. He was called from that position to Deer Lodge, Montana in the fall of 1902. There he found a high school with two teachers attempting to cover a full curriculum. That led to the organization of the Powell County High School, with four teachers and with Eaton adding the principalship to his duties as superintendent.

The pioneering venture in secondary education was moved to Trask Hall, with Eaton also living on the vacant campus. Thus, he viewed daily the abandoned facilities, remembering the colleges in the state from which he had moved, mulling over the needs of youth in this intermountain region to which he had come. Single, free from family responsibilities, he had time to brood in his dormitory room or, when sleep would come hard, wonder about what could be. So concerns became convictions and the urge to act, with the silent campus emerging as a school of dreams.

Brother Lewis later recalled the scene that led to the Eaton's engagement with Montana's educational frontier:

> In the great states of Montana, Wyoming and Idaho—an area about forty times that of Massachusetts and with a population of over a million people who were scattered over vast distances in the little mining camps and frontier settlements—there were thousands of young people growing up with little chance of receiving an education. Nothing was ever done to even arouse their ambition for higher and better living. In the few larger towns there were good high schools, but these towns were on an average of a hundred miles apart and fifty per cent of the population lived in little isolated settlements or on the lonely ranches. If a boy from one of these places would be able by some means to enter a high school, it would be necessary for him to board in some rooming house in a rough Western town without the care of a home. This meant almost certain ruin.[1]

Ernest had determined that the trustees of the College of Montana would be more than happy to provide a ten-year lease to the campus with renewal options. In search of funds for a new school, he first wrote without success to two denominational Home Missionary and Educational Societies, and then appealed to the State Superintendent of Public Instruction. That office was sympathetic, but aid to private and church-related institutions was proscribed by the Montana Constitution. Undeterred, Ernest turned to his brother, to find, somehow, within family resources the means to respond to an urgently felt need.

What happened ranks high among profiles in courage in American higher education. Lewis was now a professor and assistant to the president at Highland Park College. He had married, bought a home in Des Moines, and was loath to leave a comfortable situation. Ernest came back in 1902 to urge consideration, continued his appeals from Deer Lodge, and then returned again in 1904. The younger brother's entreaties could not be denied, and Lewis resigned his professorship, and sold his home to invest the modest proceeds in a highly risky venture in distant Montana. As further evidence of family backing, parents Thomas and Delia sold their home in Iowa and relocated in Deer Lodge. The elder Eaton invested in real estate and later, after the move to Billings, purchased a ranch at Polytechnic, Montana (west of Absarokee). He died in January, 1921.

The brothers viewed a scene that called for something of Ezekiel's vision in the Biblical valley of dry bones. Trask Hall was in fair shape, having been in recent use, but other buildings had been abandoned to the pack rats and the elements, without even the attention of a caretaker. Windows were broken and roofs in disrepair, exposing valuable contents — scientific and mining equipment, pianos, library holdings, kitchen and dining facilities for 80 boarding students—all to vandal depredations. There was little to lift the spirits of the enterprising brothers.

Undaunted, they began to make repairs, announcing in the region's newspapers on July 22, 1904 that a school would be opened on September 20th. The *First Annual Announcement of Montana College* introduced a school whose "one purpose" was "to answer the call of the great, active, practical masses...to furnish a training that fits for life" (p.3). That training would be available in several departments, namely, Commercial, Shorthand and Typewriting, Engineering, Music, Manual Training, Teaching, Academy, and Elementary Grades. In addition, a Summer Session of eight weeks would utilize frequent excursions to neighboring mountains and lakes.

Deer Lodge, it was noted for parental eyes, provided an ideal location, as a town "unusually free from the wild and unpleasant features of many western cities and its people are far above the average in intelligence and moral tone" (p.8). A town with both a public and private library, it was exceptional for its interest in education and for those things that contribute to community betterment.

With Lewis as president and Ernest as financial director, the brothers were both eager and apprehensive as September 20th came around. By that date students had arrived from 10 states, numbering nearly 100. Before the year was out, there would be more than 150 from 16 states. Lewis remembered that some had traveled by horseback over hundreds of miles across plains and mountains, then selling their ponies and saddles to cover the remaining distance by rail. "They gladly accepted the poor accommodations of those old ruins in their eagerness for an education which had been denied them."[2]

That first year had both its "highs" and "lows." There was evident need in the region for the brothers' version of practical training—"education of the three H's, the head, the heart, and the hands."[3] But student fees ($240 for room, board and tuition in any department except Music for one year of 36 weeks) fell far short of the funds needed for the new school, and that first year sorely tested the family's resolve.

The Eatons never knew from week to week if there would be resources to keep the doors open. Ernest, still single, * retained his superintendent's position and applied most of his salary to school expenses. Both brothers used all of their savings and went deeply into debt. The parents, likewise, supported their sons' undertaking. Lewis recalled that in the first winter all the dormitory rooms were taken, and he and his wife relinquished their apartment to occupy an unfinished room on the top floor.

The need for an endowment along with operating support was obvious if their school was to continue. That challenge would soon take them afield, notably back East to Chicago and New York. Meanwhile, the *Second Annual Announcement of Montana College 1905–1906* reaffirmed the brothers' educational philosophy, its focus upon practical training, competency with numbers, reading, writing, those essentials without which the students would be "unable to enter into the practical affairs of a busy world, whether it be at the carpenter's bench, the bank, the farm, the school, or the home" (foreword).

---

* Ernest married Augusta M. Valiton of Deer Lodge on September 6, 1911. They had a daughter, Margaret Louise, and son, Robert Thomas Eaton.

Their scheme for a school did not neglect extracurricular activities. Montana College offered athletics (boys basketball and football), student societies and clubs, Y.M.C.A., band, orchestra, and glee club. Life at the college was seen as happy and productive, more of a family affair with students involved in shaping the campus environment. The Eatons figured that such openness contributed to the 90 percent student return prediction for the next year.[4]

Montana College was described as "strictly non-sectarian, but thoroughly Christian." Nearly all of the faculty were active in local congregations. Church attendance was not compulsory, but students were encouraged to attend some church on a regular basis. A weekly convocation gathered students "for general exercises of an uplifting character, " along with announcements, lectures, and special entertainment.

Scant resources severely limited faculty selection. Both the president and his wife, Mary, taught courses, as did sister-in-law Emma Johnson. She would remain with the Eatons along all the way to Rocky Mountain College. Versatility was viewed as a definite asset in additions to the teaching staff. That was evident in a letter of August 9, 1905 Lewis wrote to Emma. She was in Chicago at the time preparing to direct the school's Elementary Department. He mentioned a new music teacher coming up from Denver. He was graduated from a school of Civil Engineering, with twenty years of teaching Violin, Pipe Organ, Piano, and Voice. Qualified as well in "Nature Studies, " he could also handle Gymnastics, having written several books on the subject. "I think, " the President concluded, "he will be an important addition to our faculty."[5]

The summer of 1905 brought hopes for some significant financial support. Contacts had been made with Chicago philanthropist Dr. Daniel K. Pearsons, known for his generous support of educational causes. He was especially interested in new or struggling institutions and indicated a willingness to give $25,000 towards a permanent endowment, if another $75,000 could be raised. That was his approach to other institutions to which he had donated a reported $6,000,000.

It was the beginning of a continuing relationship through the Deer Lodge years and after the Eatons moved to Billings. Happily, Dr. Pearsons' challenge was met, largely through the efforts of

Mrs. Warder I. (Alma) Higgins of Deer Lodge, obtaining pledges for $50,000. Dedicated and energetic, she served for several years as president of the college's Woman's Advisory Board.[6] Her husband was a mine operator and member of the Board of Trustees. Andrew Carnegie duplicated Pearsons' offer in March, 1907, further fueling fund raising efforts. In all, more than $200,000 was raised for rehabilitation and endowment purposes.

Ironically, the Eatons' success in fund raising undermined, in part, their stay in Deer Lodge. It led to a revival of Presbyterian interest in the college and a confrontation of educational philosophies. Early in 1907, faced with a lease on the property that limited plans for growth, the brothers agreed to placing the institution back under the ownership and name of the College of Montana. The trustees of both the old and the new schools merged into a governing board and the lease was surrendered in March, 1907.

Ernest Eaton remembered that during their absence in the East that summer unilateral changes were made in the college's character. Presbyterian preachers, it seems, steeped in more formal learning, swayed the new board to reinstate a Liberal Arts curriculum. Returning in late July, 1907, the brothers were dismayed to find that six teachers had been added to handle Philosophy, Greek, Higher Mathematics, and allied subjects, while most of President Eaton's staff had been dismissed, including his wife and Emma Johnson.

The voiding of signed contracts and the canceling of courses upon which students depended caused grave concern, resulting in a compromise. Both faculties were retained for the year, creating a major financial burden. Ernest resigned his principalship at Powell County High School to assume, without pay, added responsibilities as the college's Financial Secretary.

Outwardly, the College of Montana appeared to be on the high road to assured success as the fall term began on September 10, 1907. The August 21, 1907 *Silver State* ran a lengthy review of developments on "college hill, " praising the school for "keeping up with the times." An ordinary classical college, the paper observed with prophetic accuracy, would not attract many students, but the combination with a vocational and practical curriculum would make a big difference. The article concluded:

The College of Montana is to move right forward along the lines originally mapped out. The future is hard to discern, but there can be no question as to the successful culmination of all the plans the school has made. Certainly the present hopeful conditions are a source of great satisfaction to every one in the town and especially to those who have taken an active interest in the upbuilding.

The trustees were appreciative of the Eatons' efforts on behalf of an endowment and sounder finances generally. In their August 30, 1907 meeting, they congratulated the brothers on the successful "completion of the canvass for the Endowment." They pledged themselves "to the faithful and effective administration of the trust thus committed to us." Records indicate that the endowment was still intact in 1912.[7]

But for the Eatons Deer Lodge was no longer the scene where dreams could be explored. In addition to differences over educational aims, Lewis remembered that their plans all along called for a "good farm" and other facilities where they could "be prepared to develop various industries in order that our students could be trained to be leaders in the manifold life of the region."[8] So after prayerful consideration, they decided it was the better course to leave Deer Lodge and seek a permanent location where they could establish the school of their dreams.

DEATH OF A DREAM

The local press had little to say about the change in leadership at the College of Montana. *The Silver State* on June 3, 1908 noted that "President L.T. Eaton and E.T. Eaton desired to sever their connections with the College and presented their resignations, which were accepted by the board." The same issue announced the election of new trustees and J.H. Dickason of Wooster, Ohio as the new president. Something happened during the summer and the next school head was Reverend Henry R. Fancher of Batavia, New York. He would brave the declining fortunes of the college until 1915.

So the Eatons, undaunted by the changing circumstances, moved to the river town of Billings to pursue their dreams, to the "Magic City" as it was called by its proud citizenry. In Deer Lodge the curtain rose on the last act for the College of Montana. But there was nothing on the local scene suggesting resignation as the school opened on

September 22, 1908. Rather, *The Silver State* for the 23rd reported a good attendance, noting that there was a new shower bath in the boy's dormitory, which "will be popular with the boys, especially with the athletic squad." The larger part of the Freshman class came from the local high school.

The *Catalogue* for 1909–10 affirmed a promising future, reporting the successful conclusion of the endowment drive for $100,000. "A new era has dawned for the college. Its permanency is assured as well as the possibilities of doing better and stronger work along all lines. Advance is the watchword," (p.8). Plans for the campus included a science hall, chapel, gymnasium, more endowment, scholarships and prizes.

Joining President Fancher, M.A., D.D. were 11 colleagues and two assistants, staffing the institution's seven departments. The College offered A.B., B.S., B.L. degrees; the Academy providing preparatory schooling; the Normal Course for teachers; the Engineering Department; and the Schools of Music, Commerce and Manual Arts. In addition, a Bible Training School provided instruction in the English Bible to all college students. Its particular objectives were to prepare young men and women for careers in home and foreign missions, Sunday school and settlement work, ministerial assistance, and Y.M.C.A. and Y.W.C.A. service.

The shift back to traditional studies included the retention of Greek and Latin, particularly in the Classical Course. One is reminded of James Bryce's observation that the "small colleges are the more unwilling to drop Greek as a compulsory subject because they think that by doing so they would lose the anchor by which they hold to the higher culture, and confess themselves to be no longer universities."[9] So the little school at Deer Lodge, still a part of the Montana frontier, stayed rooted in the languages of the ancients.

While the college's nonsectarian status was maintained, there was a heavy emphasis upon nurture in the Christian faith, both in instruction and daily campus life. All students were expected to attend public worship on Sundays in the church of their choice. Also required was daily chapel and participation in Bible study. "The avowed object of the College of Montana," the *Catalogue* of 1910–11 affirmed, "is to give its students a Christian education" (p. 11). That assured the development of character, without which the acquisition of knowledge and skills had little value.

The school on the hill also aimed to provide the best of a home environment, in keeping with *in loco parentis* principles. Non-Deer Lodgers were required to live in the two dormitories, with a few exceptions for those granted permission to stay in town. Part of the tutelage was the importance of courtesy, kindness, thoughtfulness, for relationships shaped by good will. Proper manners were expected in the dining hall, where students ate their meals under a teacher's watchful eye. Conversation was encouraged as part of the social graces. The *Catalogue* for 1910–11 quoted Herbert Spencer that "to fit one for complete living is the true function of education" (p. 11).

The daily routine filled the available hours: breakfast at 7 A.M., classes from 8 A.M. to 4 P.M. with lunch at noon, dinner at 6 P.M., lights out at 10 P.M. A more leisurely Sunday schedule called for breakfast at 8 A.M., dinner at 1:30 P.M., and supper at 6 P.M. Trips off campus included study at the Kohrs Memorial Library (25,000 volumes), recitals, concerts, lectures, visiting performers (the Chicago Boys Choir was in town in April, 1910). All in all, the little village of 1,500 provided a good setting for the school.

Extracurricular activities on campus included the Isthmian Literary Society, debating and glee clubs and an orchestra; in athletics, baseball and basketball teams. The latter had won a name for itself over the state. The "young ladies" of the college were expected to take regular exercise in the temporary gymnasium. A favorite entertainment during the winter months was skating on a part of the campus flooded for that purpose. *The Collegian*, a monthly publication with student editors, reported on the various activities on the hill.

Few familiar names remained on the governing board. Banker S.E. Larabie had been with the college from the beginning. Former professor and board member Theodore Brantly continued to serve, while holding the post of Chief Justice of the Montana Supreme Court. One time German instructor and board member Eiko F. Groeneveld remained, though he had moved to Butte and to a 40-year ministry at the First Presbyterian Church. Otherwise, there were no holdovers from the earliest years. Dr. D.K. Pearsons of Chicago had replaced Adamson Trask as the school's foremost benefactor.

Mathematics class at the
College of Montana, 1907

Dr. Daniel K. Pearson

New Gymnasium in Deer Lodge, 1913

Brave talk in college publications about the future reflected the optimism of the homestead years, the near euphoria of farmers, business leaders, and the community at large that good times were here for keeps. The first issue of *The Collegian*, November, 1913, asked rhetorically "Is the college alive? For answer watch the workmen busily laying the foundation of the new gymnasium. See the bands of students hurry across the campus or hear them give the old college yell, 'U-rah-rah, Montana'" (p. 1). The student paper credited President Fancher with a veritable transformation of the bleak, dispirited campus he had found in 1908 to an attractive college home for some 150 students.

The construction of a new gymnasium in 1913 did seem to signal further progress. An anonymous Eastern gift of $10,000 had cleared the way for that much needed project. There had been some delay in building, but the new facility was opened with due ceremony on December 19, 1913. It housed a basketball court, seating for 800, swimming pool, and a visitor's gallery. The local press reported a large crowd in attendance, with music by the college orchestra and glee club, along with the usual speeches — all in dedication of "one of the finest (gymnasiums) in the West."[10] Meanwhile, the students had also built a heating-lighting plant. It was a day to indulge old dreams of Deer Lodge as a home for higher learning in Montana.

That year also saw renewed efforts for a larger endowment, sufficient to make the school self-supporting. Railroad giant James J. Hill had dangled a $50,000 challenge gift, if the college could raise another $150,000. In a promotional piece, trustees recalled the institution's heritage as the pioneer effort in higher education. They remembered those, more than 30 years ago, who first ignited the light of learning in this "Little Village on the Trail to Bear." Their vision and courage should now inspire others to give generously, in the pioneer spirit, to a school on the threshold of an even greater future.

Deer Lodge responded with pledges of around $50,000. But by 1915 the college's operations ledger was in serious imbalance. Annual deficits had contributed to a $16,000 indebtedness, with little or no growth in student enrollments. The Synod had pledged moral and financial support and "a cordial reception to our fields of labor and pulpits." Little support, however, had materialized and a joint meeting of college trustees and all Presbyterian clergy in the state was called for May 4, 1915. There were now more than 70 ministers serving 73 churches with over 5,500 members and congregational expenses nearing $100,000.[11] It was reckoning time, with church resources among the items on the table for discussion.

The Silver State for May 6th reported a spirited and harmonious occasion. President Fancher was among the missing, his recent resignation evidencing weariness with the task and desire to find other fields of endeavor. It was announced that a new leader, Franklin H. Geselbracht, would be in place for the September opening. It was also reported that some $40,000 (source not disclosed) would be available for the Board's Executive Committee to pay all bills and remodel campus buildings. It seemed like the dawning of a new day. The infusion of cash in the local economy would be appreciated by Deer Lodge businessmen who had been generous in carrying college accounts.

Following "strenuous" discussions, the clergy and trustees, wives, faculty, and students were served dinner in North Hall by the College Woman's Advisory Board. "It was," the newspaper said, "a veritable love feast." There were remarks full of "the flow of hopeful promises and bright prophesies of the future." Dr. Groeneveld was there to personalize the past, while also eloquently offering visions of things to come.

What happened to the reported $40,000 is not mentioned in available records, for a college bulletin for February, 1916 lamented the lack of funds to replace two faculty, one of whom was to serve as Acting Dean. The endowment drive had been suspended, hopefully to be renewed the following year. In lieu of extensive renovations, the Women's Advisory Board had been active decorating and partly refurnishing dormitory rooms. Their efforts were reminiscent of the earlier ladies of Deer Lodge who saw to it that Trask Hall was brought to completion.

The new president brought impressive credentials to Deer Lodge, with an A.B. from the University of Chicago, a B.D. from McCormick Theological Seminary, and a Ph.D. from the University of Leipzig in Germany. He had taught at the University of Chicago, and ministered in the city before moving to Albany, Oregon, where he served the Presbyterian church and taught Philosophy at the local college. Perhaps mercifully for him and the struggling school on the hill fate intervened the following year with America's entrance into World War I. That happened in April, 1917, followed by the Selective Service Act and the draining of student populations across the land. The prospect was too daunting, along with the competition from public schools and the long twilight struggle with finances. On the last Thursday in that April, the governing board met and voted to close the college at the end of the semester. The trustees reckoned, however, without President Geselbracht and the faculty who proceeded to resign en masse before the term was over. The Music Department was the sole exception.

Thus, the bell tolled for the final time on the once envisioned "Athens of the West." That fall high school classes were conducted on campus, while the new Powell County High School was under construction. Also, North Hall was rented out to "young ladies, " many of whom were students at the high school. In addition, a former music teacher at the college had a studio there. But these were short-term arrangements, and soon the campus was vacant as it had been at the turn of the century. Buildings would be left without maintenance, falling into disrepair. Trask Hall, that sturdy structure lasting to this day, was once again "a silent sentinel on the hill."

Total assets at the time of closing stood at over $200,000, including the endowment, four main buildings, and a campus reduced to 15 acres.[12] It was too valuable to ignore and on July 21, 1921 the trustees of School District I voted to purchase the buildings and land for $37,500, payment to be made $5,000 annually at six per cent interest. It was a particularly painful demise for the Eatons, who figured that they had personally invested $25,000 in the school. With regard to the endowment they had worked hard to raise, Ernest was unhappy that the funds had been poorly managed and lost much or all of their value. Total college assets at the time of the merger with Montana Wesleyan College creating Intermountain Union College were $54,651.43.[13] Not subject to measurement or loss was the enduring influence the school had had on hundreds of young people, either in pursuit of classical learning or vocational training, who had entered its doors.

Students at Montana Wesleyan College.

PART TWO

❖

MONTANA WESLEYAN

**The Early Years
Montana Wesleyan College
Intermountain Union College**

Original valley building used by Montana Wesleyan College.

Chapter Four The Early Years

" When this great and liberal territory has been fully canvassed...liberal philanthropists of our communion and commonwealth, in Montana and elsewhere, will endow its chairs and someday our beloved Montana Wesleyan University will be one of the largest as well as one of the best institutions of Methodism."
— *Minutes 1891 Conference*

Meanwhile, as Deer Lodge efforts collapsed, a similar venture had been struggling along in the Prickly Pear Valley. Montana Wesleyan grew from the 1877 Bozeman meeting of the Montana Methodist Conference, noted in the *Prologue*, that proved to be premature in its effort to establish a "school of higher grade." The committee appointed "with discretion to act" was able enough, representative of the best Methodist leadership in the territory. But the task at that time was an impractical one, given the vast distances, a scant, migratory population, a few overgrown villages and mining camps loosely called cities, and no railroads north of Utah or west of Bismarck. There really wasn't that much for the new conference to organize, let alone a college, with five or so preaching points, only four full-fledged ministers, and several hundred members at most.

But if the time was too soon, the intentions of the gathered few were no less real. They were deeply concerned about education for the young and, as their bishop reminded them, they belonged to a tradition that valued learning. Committee member Francis Asbury Riggin was a graduate of Dickinson College at Carlyle, Pennsylvania, an early venture for American Methodism opened in 1783. Among others, Allegheny College came along in 1816 in the same state, while

Wesleyan College was launched at Macon, Georgia in 1836 as the nation's first college for women.

West of the Alleghenies, there was Lebanon Seminary in Indiana (1828) which became McKendree College in 1834. Three years later, Asbury University was founded at Greencastle, Indiana, which later became DePauw University. Each had begun with daring talk. Others would be planted over the rugged face of the Rocky Mountain West. Paul M. Adams could understand the bold thoughts at Bozeman for a school in Montana. Admitted to the Montana Conference in 1902, the beloved professor at Wesleyan and Intermountain Union still shared the frontier spirit of building from the ground up.[1]

Years passed, however, without any definite proposals, though there were some changes in committee membership. By 1886, farmer-preacher Hugh Duncan was heading the educational effort, with Reverend George Comfort as secretary. The transplanted Scot was light on formal learning but firm in his desire that others might have the educational opportunity which had escaped him. Both he and Comfort were early arrivals in the 1860s, working on the foundations of Methodism in the territory.

The Presbyterian presence at Deer Lodge added some incentive for the Methodists to have their own school, and on May 11, 1886, the Education Committee met in Helena. A proposal was formulated that towns interested in a college location must provide no less than $50,000 in cash and subscriptions and 200 acres in land. That resulted in an offer by Helena's Fred Gamer and others of 200 acres in the Prickly Pear Valley, three miles north from town. Gamer was a local shoe merchant who would be one of Wesleyan's staunchest supporters. They attached a condition that the Conference would commit at least $10,000 over the next two years toward "improvements."

The Education Committee was not prepared to recommend the Gamer offer to the Conference in 1887; rather, still another Committee of Five was appointed, along with the presiding elders, "to whom the whole subject of education shall be referred." The new group was to confer with Gamer and others to "learn what amount of money and property can be secured in the city of Helena;...Said committee shall also use all diligence to learn what property can be secured at other places...and to report to the ensuing Conference."[2]

Lest anyone doubt the need for action, the Committee made its position clear:

> Recognizing the importance of religious and intellectual culture as an element of the highest usefulness, we strenuously reaffirm the mission of the church as an educator, and, for the collegiate grades, the *only* adequate instructor. As *ministers*, we should use every effort to impress our people with the importance and advantages of such education and the duty of providing for it.[3]

MONTANA WESLEYAN UNIVERSITY

The conversation first heard at Bozeman in 1877 finally resulted in measures taken at the Missoula Conference in 1888. By then the territorial population had topped 140,000, including 1,500 Methodists served by 26 preachers. Missoula itself signified changing times and new opportunities. Since the coming of the railroad in 1883, the "garden city" had blossomed with a populace of 7,000. The Conference resolved to establish a college, accepting the Helena offer of 205 acres lying north of the city, with the commitment to raise $50,000 for a building. Bishop Isaac W. Joyce took Reverend R.E. Smith from the Helena District Superintendency to serve as field agent for subscriptions and as the first president. The Conference subscribed $2,000 for his first year's salary.

Smith was also instructed to find a temporary location and begin some instruction that fall. As it happened, he had challenge enough in cultivating supporters. It was not the best of times for such efforts, with several fund drives afoot in the community, including one at the Methodist church. In addition, there was a presidential election underway, with powerful convictions swirling around the tariff issue, among others. Republicans had an ardent protectionist in Benjamin Harrison and were busy raising money to unseat incumbent Grover Cleveland. Actually, it was more of an excuse for not giving, as Smith noticed little change in attitudes after the election was over.

His wearisome rounds of the counting houses and business offices did produce some results. He "corralled" Samuel Hauser on a day when the capitalist-former governor was confronted with several sizable requests and was amenable to a $5,000 subscription. Fellow entrepreneur, Charles A. Broadwater, was good for another $2,500.

photo courtesy of the Archives of the
Yellowstone Conference of the United Methodist Church

Rev. Jacob Mills was a major patron of Montana Wesleyan College.

Pioneer Methodist minister and circuit rider Brother Van, was a moving spirit behind Montana Wesleyan College.

Reverend Robert P. Smith served as chancellor and representative of the board of Montana Wesleyan College.

Fred Gamer was not in their league financially, but he gave more from available resources. He donated 50 acres of land and secured subscriptions for the remainder. The shoe merchant from Baden, Germany underwrote the cost of excavations for the new building and provided the rocks for its foundations. As board member and treasurer, he would stand by the fragile school as debts mounted, investing thousands of dollars, even helping where he could after the Panic of 1893 wrecked his business. He was one of those who refused to see their little college wither and disappear. It was Paul Adams' view that "No one made a greater contribution than Gamer to the cause of Christian education in Montana."[4]

Jacob Mills was another staunch supporter. The hardy Vermonter, reared on stony, unyielding soil, Civil War veteran which cost him an arm at the Battle of Winchester, was equal both to the hardships and opportunities of the Western frontier. Successful in investments, he purchased a horse ranch in Montana, combining business activities, including sheep raising and banking, with a passion for preaching. It was the latter which really led to his relocation West in 1882 and to many years of uncommon service to Methodism in the state. Less the dreamer, more the realist, he was one who urged caution in planning and promoting the Helena school, initially voting against it. But once the decision was made, Mills was in the vanguard all the way. Over the years, he contributed $67,000 to Montana Wesleyan.[5]

There were others who responded, but no one gave more sacrificially than the ministers, surviving on salaries averaging $600 yearly, committing ten per cent to the Wesleyan cause. Each Annual Conference the appeals were renewed to give from their pittance, cultivate gifts from parishioners and preach sermons on behalf of the school. Brother Van (William Wesley Van Orsdel) never tired of urging fellow pastors to give $50 scholarships to attract students to Helena.

By the time the Conference next met in 1889, $25,000 had been subscribed. The 205 acres were valued (generously) at $35,000, placing the preliminary resources at $60,000. The plan was to sell part of the land as house lots to help finance the new institution. Such a development was currently in use at the Methodist university in Denver and seemed feasible, especially with the possibility that the street railway company might build an extension to the campus.

It was on July 6, 1889, a Saturday at 5 P.M., when Conference attendees gathered at the valley campus for the cornerstone ceremonies. The foundation was in place. Wilbur F. Sanders, president of the new board of trustees, made some introductory remarks, followed by Bishop Daniel A. Goodsell giving a prayer, reading some scripture, and wielding the trowel. Reverend W.H. Hickman, presiding elder of the Crawfordsville District, Northeastern Indiana Conference, also spoke. He was under consideration as Smith's successor in the presidency. Some in the audience questioned the wisdom of the valley location, but the mood was clearly one of celebration and anticipation of good things to come.[6]

Montana was crossing over the threshold to statehood. It was a land of boundless resources, fertile prairies, with rails connecting with distant markets. Wesleyans in Ohio, Iowa, and Illinois, among others, had grown from small beginnings within their states. So the founders in Helena thought big and named their new venture "Montana University." Nothing less would suffice for their pride, faith, and determination to succeed. Thus it was incorporated under territorial statutes. For many gathered that day, founding the school was the real crux of their faith. One building would be up and, in their view, others would follow. With the establishment of the state institutions in 1893, pressure would be applied for a name change and the little school would become Montana Wesleyan University.

For his part, Smith had had enough of fund raising and welcomed a return to the parish, this time in the Cincinnati Conference. "I have tried to do my duty, " he reasoned, "but certainly have done no more than this. Had the choice of Agent been a wiser one, greater things might have been accomplished, for if I have a special aptitude for anything it is not in my judgment along the line of begging." Yet, he was clearly pleased to have been involved in the beginnings of Methodist higher education in Montana. It was part of a denominational mission, he noted, "unrivalled in Christendom." According to his count, no fewer than 212 Methodist-related colleges and universities had been established in the past 60 years.[7]

The first board of trustees did not lack for leading citizens. Wilbur Fisk Sanders, famed from vigilante days, would serve as president from 1889 until his death in 1905. Helena attorney, territorial legislator, prominent in Republican politics, he would become a U.S. Senator. For historian-journalist Joseph Kinsey Howard (*Montana Margins*, xi), Sanders was "probably the greatest of many able men of his time, " the "most eloquent speaker during his lifetime and few have equaled him since."

Richard Lockey and Jacob Mills were vice-presidents. Born in England, Lockey had arrived in Helena in 1866, read law with Wilbur Sanders, turned to the mercantile business, then real estate, insurance, banking, mining, while also serving several terms on the city council and one in the state legislature. He was one of the few Methodist laymen of means who gave substantially to the new school. Other board members included attorney John Thompson as secretary, Fred Gamer as treasurer, future governor J.E. Rickards, and Methodist stalwarts Reverends Francis Asbury Riggin and William Wesley Van Orsdel. President Tower also served as a trustee.

J.E. Rickards was among those who added credibility to the new undertaking in the valley. The native Delawarean had moved to Butte in 1882 via Colorado and California, where he became well known in business and civic affairs. He was a delegate to the Constitutional Convention in 1889, then Lieutenant Governor in the new state establishment, next elected Governor in 1892. He served as a Wesleyan trustee for nearly 10 years, while further evidencing his confidence in the school by enrolling two sons in its first classes. Paul M. Adams wrote of Rickards and other trustees: "It was the confidence of the community in the integrity of these respected business men which kept the credit of the young institution good in these early days."[8]

BEGINNINGS ❖

Something happened with Hickman's appointment and Reverend F.P. Tower, A.M., D.D. followed Smith in the presidency. A Connecticut native, he had prepared for the Methodist ministry, been admitted to the New York East Conference in 1863, later relocated West to California and then Salem, Oregon. There he served as financial agent for Willamette University. He was called to Helena in 1889 to preside over the completion of the building in the valley, readying it for occupancy in the fall of 1890.

Early student Edward Laird Mills remembered Tower as "a good specimen of the type of college president in vogue in the last genera-tion."[9] His Phi Beta Kappa key from Connecticut Wesleyan was hardly a common possession on the Montana frontier, symbolizing the pursuit of learning to which the fledgling institution aspired. His salary may have been somewhat more than Smith's $2,000, for Gamer later reflected that "high priced presidents" had contributed to the school's growing deficits.[10]

The new structure was an impressive presence in the valley, with five floors counting the attic and basement. The latter contained the dining room, kitchen, and heating plant. Classrooms and assembly hall occupied the first floor, while the remaining three were used for dormitory purposes. The first *Catalogue* for 1891–92 advised that bathrooms on the different floors provided an adequate supply of hot and cold running water, an obvious luxury for youth from the coun-tryside. The ladies' accommodations were located on the floor beneath the gentlemen's rooms, and the sexes mingled only for dining and in the classrooms. Faculty and staff also had rooms in the building and provided supervision.

The new building had cost about $50,000, of which $35,000 had been subscribed, with some additional money raised by sale of a few house lots. The Conference fully expected to liquidate all indebted-ness "within the calendar year." Clearly, there was no shortage of hope among Wesleyan's founders:

> When this great and liberal territory has been fully canvassed ... liberal philanthropists of our communion and commonwealth, in Montana and elsewhere, will endow its chairs and someday our beloved Montana Wesleyan University will be one of the largest as well as one of the best institutions of Methodism.[11]

They sensed in the setting— "University Place"—the possibilities for real growth, for a future as wide as the mountain horizons that rimmed the Prickly Pear Valley. It made for a spaciousness of outlook. So there was bold talk of other buildings, facilities to house schools of law, mining, medicine and ministry. Their school would join the proud procession of Wesleyans that had followed the frontier westward.

Meanwhile, clergy and laity were needed to recruit students. That September, 1890, found 40 enrolled, with an average age of 18 and varying widely in their preparation for college work. From farms and ranches and small rural communities, many were still at the grade school level and required extensive remedial training. That was common early on for colleges in the West, but Montana Wesleyan would be fated for the next quarter century to function more as an academy than as an institution of higher learning. A few degrees would be conferred as harbingers of another day to come.

The first school *Catalogue* for 1891–92 detailed a curriculum designed to meet an array of educational needs. There were two departments, namely, College and Sub-College, with the first listing courses under Liberal Arts and Fine Arts headings, leading to baccalaureate degrees. The Sub-College offerings included such courses as College Preparatory, English Normal, Seminary, Industrial Scientific, Commercial, and Common School. Instruction in Music and Art was available on an individual basis. There were three terms with expenses listed as $200 for room and board and tuition from $32 to $50. All tuition and half of board and room were due in advance, with discounts for more than one student per family.

The instructional task, with its multiplicity of needs, fell to President Tower, two full-time faculty, and several part-time teachers. His areas, when not in pursuit of funds, were Ethics, Psychology, and Philosophy. J.C. Templeton, B.S. left the school superintendency in Miles City to come to Wesleyan in 1890 to teach Science and Mathematics. He would find that he had a whole "settee" of subjects. Mrs. M.S. Cummins, B.S. arrived the following year to combine Modern Languages, Latin and English with responsibilities as Preceptress. Paul M. Adams remembered that the president's son, Olin F. Tower, was also a mainstay on the faculty, though his name did not appear in the Catalogues.

In the classroom and elsewhere, the college aimed to provide youth with opportunities for "a thorough liberal education…under conditions that are best adapted to develop the worthiest character." That involved religious nurture (of a nonsectarian nature) and, accordingly, all boarding students were required to attend both Sunday morning chapel and afternoon Bible class. It was important, too, that resident faculty "earnestly endeavor to create all the elements of a refined and happy home…whose influence will do much to develop a pure and noble character."[12]

Wesleyan would have its share and more of the immature and unruly, testing its ideals, requiring stern disciplines, even expulsions, earning in some quarters the name of reform school. Meanwhile, the first year produced two women graduates, baccalaureate degrees not recorded, with Governor Joseph K. Toole as commencement speaker. Methodists seemed inclined to dismiss happenings in Deer Lodge as they celebrated the beginnings of higher education in Montana.

On the financial side, an operations deficit of $1, 600 added to a total indebtedness of $27,000. Presiding Elder S.E. Snider of the Helena District viewed the year with evident satisfaction, reporting to the Annual Conference in 1891 that "few institutions have opened under more favorable auspices than the Montana University." It surely justified for him both hope and pride, reason enough for the "hearty cooperation" of every Methodist preacher in the state. Each one was needed "in securing students and money in his charge."[13]

At the 1892 Annual Conference, the Education Committee urged each pastor to designate the first Sunday in December as "University Day, " preach an appropriate sermon on education, and take a collection or receive subscriptions for the school. Snider elaborated:

> This institution needs the hearty cooperation of every Methodist in Montana. If it can survive its infantile period and overcome the difficulties that lie in the way of a firm financial basis, or in other words, if this institution can be relieved of its burdensome debt in the near future, then we have hope of it accomplishing grand results and for this reason alone it is necessary that the Montana University have the prayers, sympathy, and cooperation of every Methodist in Montana.[14]

If finances were worrisome, as they would continue to be, Montana Wesleyan was fortunate time and again with able teachers and leaders who believed deeply in the promise of the little school. Mary Stuart Cummins was an early example. Born in Tennessee, educated in Virginia, she entered teaching, married, and moved to Helena in 1886 where she became principal of the high school. She combined broad culture and deep spirituality in ways that had a lasting influence on her students. She also traveled the state for Wesleyan, visiting in homes, a persuasive public speaker on various occasions. This talented woman later served as president of the Montana Teachers Association and the State Women's Christian Temperance Union.

Like her colleague, J.C. Templeton, she left a good position in public education to risk a career out in the valley. Besides dedicated teachers, the new institution had little to offer as a center of learning. Library resources were virtually nonexistent, while the laboratory's chief claim for equipment was a human skeleton, possibly the castoff from a mining camp, which served both for anatomy classes and Halloween pranks. But by way of some compensation, Wesleyan could boast of the view in the valley, second to none, a campus framed by the foothills of the Rockies on the West and the Belt Mountains to the East. College catalogues also noted a healthy climate, excellent for the body as well as for the mind and spirit.

"University Place" was located three miles north of town, on Montana Avenue, "a magnificent boulevard" that ran from the slopes of Helena across the valley into the foothills beyond. Paul M. Adams observed that the campus was "near enough to the city to utilize its advantages and far enough to escape its distractions."[15] At first, the miles to town represented a challenge for restless Wesleyans, solved on occasion by hitching a ride with the milk wagon on its regular routine. But then the extension of street car rails in 1892 made for easier access. The fare was ten cents each way, with commuters riding at reduced rates. Students waiting for the next car's arrival were invited to browse at the Helena Book Company or stop at Gamer's Shoe Store on Main Street.

Uniform attire identified Wesleyans in town, the boys in the military garb of the state militia and the girls in navy blue woolen suits. A vizorcap with the MWU initials survives in the Methodist Archives at Rocky Mountain College as evidence of sartorial requirements. In addition to the uniforms costing $18.00, the boys were required to purchase their own ammunition for daily target practice with muskets of Civil War vintage. A military company, sanctioned by the federal government, had been organized on campus in December, 1891, serving as a special branch of the State militia. Student officers received commissions from the governor. The 1892–93 *Catalogue* (p.29) explained that daily drill provided physical exercise equivalent to that in a gymnasium, encouraged habits of obedience to rightful authority, fostered "a manly bearing, personal neatness and self-respect, and encouraged respect for duties imposed by patriotism."

The young men viewed their uniforms as something of a nuisance when in town and preferred to conceal identity, but also rather a source of pleasure when they met girls who admired the brass buttons. Wesleyan coeds could escape their dress code by donning skirts for bicycle riding, part of the craze then sweeping the country. They had their own club and plenty of space in which to indulge a healthy pastime. As for other relaxations, early student Edward Laird Mills remembered that tennis was also a favorite activity.

EDGE OF SURVIVAL

The prospects seemed promising as "Montana University" completed its third year in June of 1893. Commencement exercises in the valley were a four-day affair, from the 11th to the 14th, and included a "University sermon" by Presiding Elder F.E. Brush, D.D., an Oration before the Pullman Literary Society by Lieutenant Governor A.C. Botkin, and another Oration by President Wilbur F. Sanders. The one-time Vigilante leader had only the brightest visions for the school, certain of state support, and that Helena, too, that "fair and thrifty hillside city" would shower upon the institution in the valley its "every benediction and grace."[16]

The moment was euphoric, if poor in prophecy, with lofty talk to match the neighboring mountains. Students had dutifully cleaned and decorated their rooms and were on their best behavior. There was a concert or two, the usual banquet, and award ceremonies for high scholarship. The new electric car line aided in bringing towns-people to University Place. The Board of Trustees was in session, finding the outlook for their fledging institution brighter than ever.

There were 130 students registered for the fall of 1893 and President Tower was busy recruiting more faculty. The Methodist Annual Conference at Bozeman in August was informed that the "last year has been the most prosperous in the history of the Institution in the number of students attending (133), in receipts and in general effectiveness."[17] The total accumulated indebtedness of $38,000 produced pledges of several thousand dollars and a resolve to mount a canvass and eliminate the problem "at an early day." As usual, the preachers with their marginal salaries were among the first to volunteer.

Storm clouds were gathering, however, that summer of 1893 when Professor J.C. Templeton journeyed to Chicago to attend the Columbian Exposition, commissioned by President Tower to purchase more furniture for dormitory accommodations. One wonders, in passing, if he met with his counterpart from the Deer Lodge college, who was also visiting the "White City" on the shore of Lake Michigan. Interestingly, there is little acknowledgment in the early Methodist accounts of the Presbyterian school.

Templeton was in Chicago when a series of bank failures and industrial collapses announced the onset of the Panic of 1893. He wired Tower for directions, whose advisors wrongly counseled that conditions were a "temporary flurry" and so the purchases were made. Of the 130 expected students, seven were present in September for the opening assembly, outnumbered by the ten faculty on the platform. Seldom, if ever, in the annals of what would become Rocky Mountain College was there a more dismal moment. Paul Adams recalled that only one student paid the full fees and in gold since all the banks were suspect. In the next two weeks, seven more students trickled in.

Still in its infancy, the fragile school faced bleak times. Banks closed across the state and businesses were near a standstill. For Jacob Mills, now the presiding elder of the Bozeman District, "The hot winds of Kansas never wilted a field of corn more quickly than has the financial stringency, in passing over our state, disarranged all calculations in money matters."[18] Plotted houselots at University Place with their hoped-for income now sold for a song or would revert to ranch land of minimum value.

Dispirited trustees, burdened with their own personal problems, met in an emergency session and accepted president Tower's recommendation that only Templeton and Mrs. Cummins be retained in a skeleton operation to finish the year. They would receive half-salary in cash and the remainder in university lots. They would have three student assistants and be guaranteed against loss in the boarding operations. President Tower would search for funds in the East, while released faculty found various employment. It had been an especially grievous summer for Tower whose wife, Julia, died following a long illness.

Enrollment grew that year to 32 students, thanks in large part to Templeton and Mrs. Cummins devoting weekends to recruiting around the state. With close management, church collections of $650, and some donations the current bills were met. Tower's resignation (1889–1894) and return to the pastorate back East brought a four-year contract for the hard working team. Trustees guaranteed them against personal loss, while providing that they would retain all income above expenses. They were authorized to hire any additional teachers, pay the bills, and generally assume responsibility for operations. This arrangement was modified in 1895 to provide that one-third of all net income over $2,400 would revert to the governing board. In all, over their tenure, Templeton would receive $5,670 and Mrs. Cummins $5,153.[19]

The young man from Missouri and his able, dedicated colleague served the struggling school well, keeping the doors open through the most austere of times. Only grudgingly did the Panic of 1893 release its grip upon the land. But Templeton, like Mrs. Cummins, was seasoned for such an assignment, the product of country schools in Kentucky to which his family had moved, working his way through Elkton Academy and the National Normal University at Lebanon, Kentucky. Along the way, as early as age 18, he had been in full charge of a district school. He had come to Miles City as a school superintendent in 1888, then joined the first Wesleyan faculty two years later. Following his Montana stay, he would study at Stanford University and then teach in California and Nevada.

Enrollment fluctuated during the Templeton-Cummins years, from 32 in 1892–93 to 82 in 1895–96 to 46 in 1897–98. The average age also varied from 16 to 18. Not more than 25 per cent of the students had come prepared for high school work or anything beyond. Schooling for many from the countryside had been limited to shortened terms, with frequent absences to do farm chores. Grown youth working with the basics often made for disciplinary problems. In his final report to the Wesleyan Board (Conference *Official Journal* 1901), Templeton urged "a standard of maturity and scholarship below which the school will not drop even for the sake of much needed revenue; otherwise, it must continue to grow more and more into a seminary or private asylum for the immature and undeveloped."

State pressure, along with the character of the student body, forced a name change from Montana University to Montana Wesleyan University, still a fond dream of things to come. By whatever name, parents were grateful for the opportunities the school provided, especially the emphasis upon family values and religious training. As a matter of fact, Templeton kept a yearly record of the number of Christian conversions among his charges. Adams remembered:

> Faculty and student body were small and all lived in the same building. They got to know each other intimately and the aim was to make their associations a large happy family. In most cases the plan succeeded and school life was pleasant. Each year one or more incorrigibles were suspended and expelled. In view of the small enrollment and the need for income, this was an heroic measure. Religious services were held, there were chapters of the Epworth League and of the Y.M.C.A. It was planned to throw a religious environment about the students and during the year to bring as many as possible into a definite Christian experience.[20]

Wesleyan was not alone in admitting poorly prepared students. The same was true at the Presbyterian college in Deer Lodge, and the state university system had similar remedial programs in the early years. Adams shared with Templeton a concern that the presence of so many immature students discouraged attendance by others ready for college work. Meanwhile, Wesleyan was saddled with unpaid obligations on the building. Construction and related costs had amounted to about $50,000, of which $25,000 had been subscribed but only about half that sum collected. Hard times took their toll. Money had been borrowed to pay the contractor, with the ever faithful Messrs. Gamer and Lockey pledging property as collateral.

The Conference in its August meeting in 1895 obtained subscriptions of several thousand dollars, and then in 1896 supported the Wesleyan trustees in a bond issue of $50,000. Payable in five years, the bonds carried 6 per cent interest, guaranteed by the Conference and the North Montana Mission, the other jurisdiction within Montana Methodism. College property provided security along with the "moral obligation" of the Methodist Episcopal Church. The bonds sold within the year in amounts ranging to $5,000. Gamer, Lockey, and Mills purchased the latter issue and returned them to the school, reducing the obligation to $35,000. That eased finances, but it was only buy-ing time, for another day of reckoning would come with bond redemptions in 1902.

RELOCATION AND RENEWAL ▨

Another crisis in leadership came with the resignations of J.C. Templeton and Mrs. Cummins in 1898. They had labored valiantly for five years against daunting odds, but now weary with the task, had other paths to follow. Edward Laird Mills spoke for many when he remarked that Montana had had no better teachers. Paul Adams could name a number of their students who later became prominent in various professions. Templeton urged Wesleyan trustees to resume management of the college and they accepted new leadership with Dr. Thomas Van Scoy, Dean of Portland University in Oregon which had just closed its doors.

The experienced educator from Indiana was willing to try again with another school struggling to survive. With degrees from North-western University and Garrett Biblical Institute, he had served for 11 years as president of Willamette University at Salem, Oregon before his assignment in Portland. The seasoned, energetic Van Scoy proceeded to strengthen the curriculum, moving it toward collegiate quality. That first year there were five graduates with baccalaureate degrees. Enrollment was up, income the best yet, trustees and Conference in a mood to congratulate their new president for "handling the work with great skill."[21]

Life at Montana Wesleyan continued to stress the "happy home" atmosphere, with most faculty and families residing in the one build-ing, eating with students, encouraging "cheerfulness" and good manners at meals. The president's accommodations were in another large home structure, which also housed the 1,000 volume library. Participation was encouraged in the school's literary society and athletic teams (football, basketball, tennis). Tuition, board, and room at $275 per year included a 15-day trip through Yellowstone National Park. According to the 1898 *Catalogue*: "Experienced cooks accompany each party and furnish a table menu that is not excelled at any hotel, east or west" (154). Wall tents with carpets and good mattresses assured the best of sleeping in the crisp mountain air.

Van Scoy soon shared Dr. Tower's earlier dissatisfaction with the valley setting. It made sense to them that an in-town location would attract more Helena students. The 3 miles from the city became a greater problem with the removal of the streetcar tracks in 1899. Hopes for a real estate development at University Place had dimmed, and the car company used the rails to connect the city with the smelter east of town. That meant long rides in horse drawn conveyances for students, with all deliveries, including coal, adding costs for needed supplies. Then the burning of the building housing the president's family reinforced the decision to relocate in Helena.

The trustees agreed with Van Scoy and property was acquired in the city. Fund raising efforts had included $9,000 designated for that purpose. Wesleyan's new address was on Helena Avenue and the corner of Warren Street, the old German Turnverein building, vacant since the Panic of 1893. Also acquired was an apartment house on nearby Ewing Street for student accommodations, named for Jacob Mills. The solid, sandstone structure with Gothic entrance would be the school's home for the next 15 years, its gymnasium, social hall, bowling alley and basement areas converted into classrooms, laboratories, library, and auditorium.

Thus it was with the barest of essentials that Montana Wesleyans proceeded with the educational task, in the best tradition of Mark Hopkins, with teacher and student sharing a log. Paul Adams remembered that his laboratory in the basement had been a barroom. The bar was still there and served as a laboratory table for his chemistry students. He stored supplies, what few he had, in an old vault, which once had held the inventory of beer and whiskey.[22]

Despite its obvious limitations, trustees called their new acquisition "College Hall" and proceeded with dedication services. Loyal supporters gathered on a Saturday afternoon, August 11, 1900 to hear Senator Wilbur F. Sanders, still president of the governing board. Other speakers included Dr. James M. King, Secretary of the Church Extension Society of Philadelphia, Dr. H.K. Carroll, representing the Methodist Missionary Society, and Bishop Charles H. Fowler who dedicated the old hall to "high and holy uses." President Van Scoy had reason that day to be pleased with developments during his short stay in Helena and what the future might hold.

More students were enrolling, despite competition from the state institutions at Missoula, Bozeman, Dillon and Butte. The Presbyterian college in Deer Lodge had closed, but the Southern Methodists had an academy in Stevensville. Not the least of Van Scoy's contributions was adding to the faculty two former students at Portland University. Charles Wesley Tenney and Mary Eva Foster would have a deep and lasting influence on Montana Wesleyan. A missionary in Singapore before her health failed, Mary taught English and German, but it was her warm personality and compassionate nature that meant so much to her students. Their expressions of caring in the pages of *Prickly Pear*, the college annual, reflected a major influence for the good. Following a 20-year stay, she married and moved away.

Charles Tenney taught Civics and Economics. Another strong and winsome personality, he would figure prominently in Wesleyan's survival following Van Scoy's sudden death in 1901. In February the energetic president preached at Oakes Street Church in Helena, warmed to the task, then walked in subzero weather the half-mile to his home. He became severely chilled, developed pneumonia and, at age 53, was gone in a few days. It was a devastating blow to a school just sensing something of its possibilities, so much in need of what he had to offer. Tributes at his funeral were given by trustees Mills, Van Orsdel, and Ex-Governor Rickards, along with future president Charles L. Bovard. An honor guard of Wesleyan cadets led the procession to the cemetery.* Mrs. Jesse Van Scoy stayed on at her husband's school, teaching Mathematics and French.

What might have been is ever a matter of wonder, beyond the historian's ability to relate. Numbed by Van Scoy's loss, the trustees turned to one of their own, Reverend George D. King, to serve out the year as acting president. An original board member, he was well educated and well read but lacking in sufficient good health to consider extended responsibilities. That task was given to another minister, Reverend James W. Morris, Ph.D., Pastor at Kalispell, who resigned after one year in the presidency. He opted for a career as an evangelist. Once more leadership was at the crux of Montana Wesleyan's future.

---

* An engraved memorial tablet at College Hall, now in the Rocky Mountain College Archives, evidences the high student esteem for their president.

Compounding the crisis as the new century opened was the due date for the bonds issued earlier. They would mature in 1902. Thanks to Gamer, Lockey, and Mills the obligation was for $35,000, but there was also a floating debt of $10,588 to consider. Hopes were high that the Conference's participation in national Methodism's *20 Million Twentieth Century Fund* would eliminate financial worries and provide some much-needed endowment. Montana's goal in the campaign was $120,000, with the college to receive $75,000. The Conference had appointed Reverend Leaming H. Mickel as its financial agent to work towards that goal.

The Annual Meeting at Bozeman in early August, 1902 determined not only the handling of bonds but the very future of Montana Wesleyan. Trustees had come prepared to settle obligations for 50 cents on the dollar as a realistic solution, given available resources. Bond-holders present were not happy, and it was a stormy session at the church on Olive Street where talk of a college had first been heard back in 1877. Fortunately, Dr. Edmund F. Mills, national Secretary of the Twentieth Century Fund, was present to offer sage counsel and a moderating influence. Eventually bond holders agreed, including the ministers whose average salary at the time was under $650 annually. The sticky task of informing remaining bond-holders fell to an ailing Leaming H. Mickel, who accomplished it with a minimum of friction. He was another of the unsung heroes of the time.

The larger issue concerned the future of the school. There were those present, burdened not only with matters financial, but troubled by Van Scoy's passing and Morris's recent resignation, who felt that the time had come to close the doors. As on other occasions when the will weakened, it would be the pleading of an unlettered "Bro. Van," along with other stalwarts in the ranks, that carried the day. The trustees, too, had another plan for survival, namely, turning to Charles Tenney with a proposal similar to the one Templeton and Mrs. Cummins had received. The board would be responsible for recruiting students, while he would be in charge of operations and receive net profits. In addition, there would be a $500 guarantee as long as the enrollment stayed under 50 paying students. The governing board would handle repairs and retain supervision of "decorum, management and rules of discipline."[23]

Paul Adams, "the Beloved Prof," served both the Wesleyan and Intermountain Union College.

Mary Eva Foster was a major influence in teaching and administration during the early years.

Charles A. Bovard's 5-year presidency from 1911–1916 helped to develop Montana Wesleyan College.

Paul Adams with students.

The Academy ❂

Wesleyan trustees continued to refer to their "university, " cling-ing precariously to the 15 baccalaureate degrees that had been awarded among the 700 students to date. That included four in the Class of 1901. Only 27 had received diplomas from the Academy (*Catalogue*, 1901–2, 230). That was a rather meager harvest for 12 years of effort, even for the Montana frontier. Interestingly, advertisements for 1902 mentioned only the Academy of Montana Wesleyan University with its courses along with Commercial and Music offerings. The latter attracted local students and helped significantly with the enrollment.

Competition for Helena students came from a good high school and two business schools. In addition, some Methodist families were continuing to send daughters to Roman Catholic institutions as safer environments. That brought a stinging rebuke in 1903 from the Conference's Education Committee, echoing the sentiment first heard at Bozeman in 1877, that "No Protestant young man or woman can remain under the instruction of these people for a period of six months or a year and return home untainted by the insidious doctrines of the Romish church."[24]

Charles Tenney welcomed his appointment, undaunted by the struggle for students and the odds against building a solid collegiate program. A native of Vancouver, Washington, he held degrees from Willamette University (Ph.B.) and George Washington University (A.M.). Young, energetic, personable, popular with the students, Tenney was well-received by the governing board, and the arrangement would continue until 1911 when he became vice president with the trustees resuming control under Dr. Charles Bovard. Meanwhile, he would take a year off in 1907 for study back East. He left Wesleyan in 1913 to take a position with the State Department of Public Instruction supervising high schools. Later he was lured to Gooding, Idaho and a futile effort to mother a Methodist college there.

In 1905, Wesleyan trustees and the Conference added to the school's leadership team. Reverend Robert P. Smith had been trans-ferred in 1902 from his Dillon pastorate to St. Paul's in Helena, and in the summer of 1905 assigned additional duties as chancellor. He was to be the Board's representative, with salary of $2,000 paid by the trustees, with responsibilities for recruitment, fund raising, and searching for a permanent campus location in Helena or elsewhere. Smith was no stranger to Wesleyan, having taught there in 1895. Ill health forced his return to the pastorate, but he retained the post in English Literature pending a possible return to teaching. An Ohio native and graduate of Ohio Wesleyan, he was credited with being one of Montana Methodism's "clearest thinkers."

Smith was also charged with improving Wesleyan's image in the state and in that regard, proceeded to launch in 1905 a monthly publication *The Messenger*. Tenney, Adams, Edward L. Mills and others joined him in what became the official organ of Montana Methodism for the next 20 years. While Tenney managed school operations, Smith traveled the state with such energy and diligence that enrollments steadily increased, crowding College and Mills Halls, adding to trustee concerns for a larger campus.

Another newcomer in 1905 was Reverend Paul M. Adams, destined to serve Wesleyan and Intermountain Union College for the next 30 years under nine presidents, the "beloved prof" of students' recollection. A native of Illinois with B.A. and M.A. degrees from Northwestern University, he arrived in Montana in 1902 to serve churches at Virginia City and then Utica, before joining the Wesleyan faculty. His teaching areas were Mathematics and Science, but like Templeton before him, he had a whole "settee" of subjects, being drafted on occasion to handle Psychology and English.

The versatile Adams was a good match for the time and the place. When need arose, he added administration to his responsibilities, serving several years as vice president and one as acting president. He helped with *The Messenger* and, over the years, filled various posts with the Methodist Conference. He was a persuasive voice for Wesleyan, whether supplying pulpits or arguing the school's case at Conference time. His book, *When Wagon Trails Were Dim*, and his manuscript survey of Wesleyan and Intermountain Union are valuable resources for an account of their stories.

That year of 1905 found some 70 students enrolled in the Academy, taking mainly a secondary school curriculum, with remedial work for the poorly prepared, and instruction in the Commercial and Music Departments. The latter were of especial interest to Helena students and accounted for many registrations. It would be another 10 years, however, before the governing board considered a four-year collegiate program. Even then, there were those who questioned such a move.

Meanwhile, the little school was not lagging in activities, apart from classroom hours. Wesleyan students won the State Oratorical prize in 1905, placed well in debate and athletic contests (football and basketball), maintained a cadet band and drill company, a Y.M.C.A., a prayer group with 14 conversions in 1905, and a literary society. In addition, Wesleyans conducted weekly religious services at the County Poor Farm.

Adams remembered that the cadet corps still had an especial appeal for the young men. Clad in the State Militia uniform, they drilled each afternoon, equipped with old Civil War muskets. Participation was required, including the purchase of their uniforms and ammunition. Drills involved marching around town, augmented with overnight hikes to more distant locations. Cadet officers held commissions from the governor's office. Later, with the onset of World War I, some Wesleyan cadets became officers in the U.S. army.

Adams also recalled that life for residential students was rather regulated and "according to the book." Day began with Reveille at 6:30 A.M. with a designated bugler arousing the sleeping, first at the boys' dormitory and then at the girls'. Following breakfast at 7:00 A.M. rooms were to be cleaned for inspection at 8:30 A.M. Classes were held from 9:00 A.M. until noon, with a daily break for chapel. Faculty took turns, along with visiting clergy in leading devotions. After lunch, there was military drill for the young men and then afternoon classes. There was some leisure time before and after dinner at 5:30 P.M. Study hours resumed at 7:00 P.M. with lights out by 10:00 P.M.

Weekends offered more freedom for Wesleyans, though there were the Methodist cautions about dancing, card games, movies, and similar diversions. Helena's "seamy side," its numerous saloons and sprawling red light district, posed a danger for student morals and required a worried president and vice president to spend hours patrolling the streets for wayward charges. Unlike the young men, the young ladies were required to obtain the preceptress's permission to visit in town and often had chaperones.

A move into town in 1900 located Montana Wesleyan College in the old German Turnverein building renamed College Hall.

Montana Wesleyan College faculty, 1914–15.

Students patronized lectures and concerts in the city auditorium, attended athletic contests, and enjoyed "plunge parties" at the elaborate Broadwater Natatorium west of town. Another favorite activity was picnicking on Mount Helena or other scenic spots. State Fair Week in early fall brought family and former students back to campus and added to the excitement of beginning another school term. Adams could reflect: "With all its restrictions life at Wesleyan was by no means dull and in general the students acquired a genuine fondness for the institution."[25]

Wesleyans fared fairly well in that other important aspect of campus life spent in the dining hall. Meals were plain but plentiful, featuring an abundance of meat and vegetables. Occasionally some cook would overdo the soggy starches and court the displeasure of both students and faculty who ate with them. Confronted with such a meal, one professor prayed: "O Lord, grant that we may not starve in the midst of plenty." A replacement was hired the next day.[26] Students worked in the dining hall or kitchen to help with room and board at $118 per semester. Tuition was $21.50 with extra fees for music lessons.

Religion anchored much of student life and learning, faith mainly of the Methodist persuasion. In addition to the weekday chapels, there was required church attendance on Sundays, mostly at St. Paul's, where students attended Sunday School and participated in the Epworth League for youth. The church's annual revivals helped with the school's objective to record a number of conversions each year. The Conference *Official Journal* for 1905 (pp. 48-49) noted with approval that, "The religious interest was good and fourteen of the young people were converted."

A New Policy

Robert Smith's appointment as Chancellor was one of several actions taken at the Conference Meeting in Dillon in August, 1905. Delegates had come with Wesleyan's future high on the agenda, concerned that the "hour had come for initiating a new policy," including the purchase of "a new property that shall be an honor to our Church and indication of our aspiration."[27] So the first day they created a Special

Policy Committee to prepare recommendations on the school's future for Conference consideration before they left town.

Four days later, the Committee's report included the following: continue the school; obtain a permanent location in Helena or elsewhere; conduct the school as an Academy, one of outstanding quality ranking with the Wilbrahams in Massachusetts; sell the valley and Helena properties and invest proceeds in a new campus; raise $4,000 annually from the churches to implement advancement plans, including the Chancellor's salary and travel expenses; define the Chancellor's duties in public relations, recruitment, and fund raising; and solicit the full support of the clergy.[28]

Improved finances were also part of the mood to move Wesleyan forward. The bonded obligation was gone and the outstanding indebtedness was down to $8,625. Assets of $39,380 included the Henry Klein bequest, originally of $5,000 but which had tripled in value. The pioneer Jewish merchant's generosity helped greatly in meeting deficits, buying new furniture and equipment, and purchasing the campus which would bear his name. The Conference, too, was in better shape to provide support, now with 4,770 members in 90 churches served by 75 ministers. The meeting at Dillon voted a $1.00 per member sustenance fund which, however, proved hard to raise.

Reverend Edward Laird Mills, Jacob's son, was a prime mover of the new advancement policy. An early student at the school in the valley, he had replaced Smith as pastor of St. Paul's Church and also had been elected to the Wesleyan board. With Wilbur Sander's death in 1905, Mills was named president. He had completed his college work at Connecticut Wesleyan and his ministerial training at Boston University School of Theology. He had returned to Montana in 1902, pastoring at Stevensville before moving to Helena. Later, the capable Mills would serve as a District Superintendent in Montana and Utah and on the national Board of Education. Father and son contributed greatly to the survival and growth of the little school in Helena.

Chancellor Smith also was effective in breathing life into the new advancement policy. While Tenney cared for internal school operations, he traveled extensively throughout the state, utilizing trains, stage coaches, private conveyances, undaunted by Montana's capricious weather. It was not uncommon for him to speak two to four times on Sundays. Back home, there were the general business affairs of the school to be handled, including some disciplinary matters, catalogues to be reviewed and mailed, numerous promotional pieces to be written and distributed, editing the *Messenger* and so on. Sickness in his family contributed to a rather exhausting routine.

The columns of the *Messenger* promoted the school's advantages and helped to fill Mills Hall in a year or two and crowd other facilities. Dormitory spaces were added with the purchase of a private dwelling on Rodney Street. "Prexy Flats," to be used for presidential housing, also had rooms for girls and was the most popular of the dormitory accommodations. Enrollment climbed to over 180 students, where it remained for several years.

Successful in recruitment, Smith turned in 1907 to a campaign for $100,000 for a building and an endowment, operating now as Wesleyan's new president. Tenney had been granted a study leave back East. Smith proceeded in speeches and in the *Messenger* to envision a greater institution, one worthy of early dreams, the only Methodist college within an immense territory, whose Montana towns and cities were generally poised for growth.

Meanwhile, the search for a new campus ended with a tract of land in town, located north and east of the capitol building. It had been subdivided and added to the city. Old college friends Richard Lockey and Timothy Collins assisted in the purchase of several lots (28 acres), for $4,000, the amount remaining in the Klein legacy. It would be a strategic location, with Eleventh Avenue running through, providing access from East and South. With mountain vistas aplenty, it would be regarded by visitors as the most beautiful campus in all Methodism. Friends of the college were encouraged by the land purchase to pledge $15,000 to the advancement program.

The disposition of the valley property also had been an agenda item for several years. Deteriorating with the seasons, it was widely referred to as "Methodism's folly." Attempts to sell it to various parties had all misfired, including to the government for an Indian school, Odd Fellows for a retirement home, and the Catholics. The asking price of $20,000 may have been too high, but the trustees figured that was half or less of what it had cost them to build it. Finally, in 1908, the building with 14 acres was leased to the Deaconess Board

Mills Hall was the first resident hall for women in Helena.

for a children's school. The fond hope was that its graduates would matriculate later at Wesleyan. Adams observed that few of them ever did enroll.[29]

Just as Smith had momentum building, he received an offer for the presidency of Kansas Wesleyan University. A daughter's health needs for a climate change weighed heavily in his decision to accept the position and, with evident regret, he made the move. His *President's Report* of May 26, 1908 found Wesleyan still operating as an academy, with additional courses in Normal, Commercial, Music, and Elocution. Faculty salaries ranged from $35 to $75 per month, with board and room provided for the family. Smith noted that all salaries had been paid on time.

School facilities were being fully utilized by 183 students. College and Mills Halls had received much-needed improvements, with electricity replacing kerosene lamps, and new furniture for the old and badly worn. Very importantly, there was no indebtedness; in fact, significant sums were at hand for the new campus. "Public confidence in the institution," he noted, "has been restored, our credit in the city and elsewhere has become gilt edged, and there is now a bright promise that the school will enter upon an experience altogether new—freedom from debt."[30]

Regrettably, that was not to be, but the trustees must have arisen that day as one and applauded the words of their departing leader. Montana would see the Robert Smiths again. The years away were good, bringing national recognition, literary output, and travel abroad. But homing instincts brought him back in 1915, this time to the Methodist church in Bozeman where he served for 15 years. Smith combined those qualities of leadership Wesleyan badly needed— scholarly ways, vision, organizational skills, accomplished in communications, energy to pursue his dreams.

Wesleyan was fortunate in attracting several able presidents, but their stays were too short to provide that continuity in leadership essential in the advancement of an institution. Meanwhile, Charles Tenney was enjoying his stay back East, hoping for another year of graduate study at George Washington University. He was pursuing work in Law and Economics, along with a pastorate in Chevy Chase outside of Washington. It was a different scene, all of the opportunities a big city offered. But he could not deny the urgent calls from Helena, and with characteristic generosity of spirit he returned home. Paul Adams stood by as his Assistant with responsibilities for internal management, while Tenney took over the advancement program Smith had inaugurated.

That endeavor benefited from a visit in August, 1910 by Dr. Thomas Nicholson, Secretary of the Methodist Board of Education. Raised in the West, a former president of Dakota Wesleyan University, he had more than a passing interest in schools like Wesleyan. So he stayed ten days in Helena, developing plans for the Klein campus. New facilities with needed endowments called for at least $250,000, including an administration and class room building at $50,000. The campaign would cover five years, with appeals not only to the churches but to the business community in Helena and beyond.

Jacob Mills pledged $10,000 towards the first building, if the Helena community could raise $20,000 and the churches an equal amount, plus working on needed endowments. Progress was slow with only $15,000 committed by year's end. Meanwhile, talk of the new campus stirred hopes for a full collegiate curriculum. The younger Mills was impatient to begin as soon as the administration building was ready, but the trustees settled on 1916 as the more feasible time.

Dr. Nicholson was back in 1911 to check on developments, accompanied by his assistant, Dr. John W. Hancher. At the Annual conference in Billings, the advancement program was vigorously promoted. Assembled pastors caught the spirit and committed to pledging 8 percent of their salaries to Wesleyan work. Hancher was impressed, remarking that it was "one of the most heroic acts he had ever seen."[31]

That same year brought changes in Wesleyan leadership, with Reverend Charles L. Bovard named to the presidency. Tenney remained in charge of daily operations until his resignation in 1913. Paul M. Adams also returned to the pastorate. Born on an Indiana farm, of Huguenot descent, Bovard was one of six brothers to enter the Methodist ministry. Two served as presidents of the University of Southern California. His pastorates in Montana were at St. Paul's in Helena and Mountain View in Butte. Following transfers to Ohio and North Dakota, he was back in Montana by 1910 to serve one year as Superintendent of the Helena District and then the Wesleyan presidency.

Bovard brought to his new post winning ways of personality that made friends his school badly needed. Adams remembered him as a scholar and "a pulpit orator, a voracious reader and tenderhearted."[32] He also had no doubts about priorities, concluding a report to the Conference with this admonition:

> The lesson is this. Build an endowment. And until such endowment can be had, secure a pledged band of sustainers. I give you now my deepest convictions in reference to our school situation. We must bend all our energies to the task of building, and endowing our University, or lose our leadership in this great state.[33]

It would be during his five year tenure in office that Wesleyan would finally come of age as a college, a quarter-century after the laying of the first cornerstone out in the valley.

President Leon H. Sweetland's tenure, 1917–1919 saw the completion of the new Mills Hall.

President Charles M. Donaldson served the college from 1919–1923 and saw the final years for Montana Wesleyan College before the merger.

Helena Hall was the first building on the Klein Campus. It housed administration and classrooms.

Chapter Five

Montana Wesleyan College

" The most encouraging thing I know of is the work that is actually being done. Year in and year out, the school is a blessing to scores and hundreds of boys and girls."
— *Edward Laird Mills*

Changing times at Wesleyan coincided with one of Montana's greatest surges in prosperity and growth. People from Maine to the Middle Border and abroad took up homesteading in the state. The boom years were from 1910 to 1918, when some 32 million acres were put into production. The Enlarged Homestead Act of 1909 doubled the land grant to a half-section, while the Three-Year Homestead Act of 1912 limited the "proving up" period to three years. Such legislation fed railroad promotions of an agricultural Eden in the high plains. Homestead towns mushroomed on the treeless prairies, with churches multiplying along with the grain elevators. Methodists were in the vanguard, along with Lutherans, and Catholics, among others.

Seldom, if ever, have Montanans viewed the future more hopefully. Optimism rippled throughout the economy and set the tenor of the times. Wesleyans were renewed in the mission of a Christian college that mattered to the quality of life in the state. If the past 20 years had tested the will to survive, they had also produced 900 students and more, many of whom were well established in business, the professions, agriculture, and other occupations. Some had become prominent in state affairs.

One who knew the story well was Reverend George Logan, pioneer school teacher and beloved pastor. "Dad" Logan figured that Wesleyan had prepared at least 40 ministers for work in the Northwest and elsewhere, numerous others for church vocations and missions, along with the many who carried the influence of a capable and dedicated faculty into the main streams of daily life. He was confident that his "first class little school" had been for the good. And the door stood open to greater usefulness.[1]

THE BOVARD PRESIDENCY

With Charles Tenney handling daily operations for 180 students, President Bovard worked from an office in town to promote the building and endowment campaign. Two visitors in Helena that fall of 1911 would provide a boost for his efforts. Former U.S. Vice-President Charles W. Fairbanks (1904–1908) urged citizens, notably the business community, to support the school. He also visited the campus and spoke at chapel. A graduate of Ohio Wesleyan University, his presence evidently was of material benefit to the campaign. Helena contributed $50,130 to the new building, with another $5,575 coming from other towns.

The other visitor was railroad giant James J. Hill, who was in town to speak at the State Fair. He was known for his interest in small denominational colleges, specifically in their endowment needs. Bovard followed up with a visit to St. Paul in April, 1912. It was Hill's judgment that schools like Wesleyan needed an endowment of at least $300,000, and he agreed to pledge $50,000 contingent upon the remainder being raised by May 1, 1914. That commitment was featured in campaign materials as an important reason why others should participate.

Meanwhile, funding for the new building, to be called Helena Hall, included support by the faculty. Members gave from their meager resources an average of at least $100 each. That was at a time when they were earning less than the miners and bar maids in Butte. So they had a real investment in the work that began in November, 1912, with cornerstone ceremonies the following May. Occupancy came in January 1914, signaling a new day and a time for rejoicing in the life of Montana Wesleyan. Adams remembered that the two-story brick building "was modern in every way," with maple floors, tile roof, and slate blackboards from a quarry north of town. Its structure seemed solid enough, but it would be tested and found wanting in the earthquake of 1935.

Helena's response and Hill's commitment provided strong incentives for what was now termed the "Forward Movement." With Dr. Hancher's assistance, Wesleyan trustees engaged Mr. Charles Strader of Lincoln, Nebraska to manage the endowment campaign. The Methodist businessman had recently completed a successful drive for Nebraska Wesleyan University. During the fall of 1913, key workers and clergy held banquets in Missoula, Butte, Anaconda, Dillon, and Ronan. Strader was joined by Edward L. Mills, Dr. Thomas Nicholson and W.W. Van Orsdel in urging support for the campaign. As usual, "Brother Van" was the optimist:

> If it has been possible to keep Montana Wesleyan going for more than a fifth of a century when the state was sparsely settled an Methodists were few and poor, how comparatively easy it will be in new and more favorable conditions to expand our activities and build broad foundations for the future years. One half the zeal, consecration and persistence shown by our fathers will give to us a shining success in the pending campaign....Let every man be found at his post.[2]

Despite stirring campaign appeals, the fall of 1913 produced a net of only $25,931 for endowment purposes, well below expectations, and with 60 per cent coming from the Butte District. Methodists in the mining city were to be commended, for they were also involved in building a Deaconess hospital. Doubtless, the construction project had taken most of the available funds in Helena. Harsh winter conditions hampered travel around the state, restricting in particular President Bovard's activities. By spring, Jacob Mills was again encouraging endowment efforts with an offer to give $10,000 as the last of $75,000 to be raised.

Unfortunately, there were no other Jacob Mills to infuse the "Forward Movement" with large donations. Early on Messrs. Gamer and Lockey had given generously and Henry Klein had made his bequest, but over the years Mills was the only substantial benefactor. Son Edward noted that not "a single Methodist layman has been found to give more than $1,000 in the past decade, and less than five willing to give that amount."[3] During that time, he observed, a number of wealthy Montana stockmen with Methodist connections had passed on without any provisions for the school. That had to change if Wesleyan was to grow.

Another obstacle to matching Hill's or Mills' offer was Wesleyan's reputation as a preparatory school attracting poorly prepared youth from rural areas. That limited its appeal for major donors more interested in collegiate institutions and also its leverage with national church sources. The Methodist denomination's University Senate had standards which had to be met for recognition. Endowment needs continued to weigh heavily upon Bovard and his successors. Board chair Edward Mills noted in 1915 that an endowment of $50,000, if it could be raised, would help trustees balance the annual budget.[4]

The churches were the main support for current operations, beyond tuition at $25.00 per semester and board and room at $23.00 monthly. There were additional charges for Music and Expression lessons. The clergy made commitments at Conference to the "sustenation fund," pledging 8 per cent of their cash salaries, but not all were equally diligent in following through. Younger members, here for short stays, had ties with other institutions and did not fully share the Wesleyan dream. At home they met apathy from parishioners who paid taxes to support state schools and, despite Methodist affiliation, saw no reason for a double educational system. Each year in a school budget averaging $16,000, there were accumulating deficits of around $2,500.

The high point of the Bovard presidency came with the move to the Klein campus in 1914, mixing excitement for the new with strong attachments to old College Hall, fond citadel of learning for Wesleyans since 1900. Women students remained in residence at Mills Hall, while the young men roomed in private homes and took their meals with the women. It was about a mile to the new Helena Hall, made either by foot risking winter chills and snows and spring rain and mud or by the often-undependable street car. Either way, the students had lunch in the basement of their new building.

That fall of 1914 brought a number of promising young students demanding college work. They were mostly Methodist in background and wanted to make things happen at the school. Paul M. Adams had returned the previous year as Vice President and, with colleagues, responded with a curriculum for Freshmen and Sophomores. The Board pledged a full 4-year program for 1916. Few in number but mature and well motivated, these students proceeded to provide leadership and an atmosphere befitting a college scene. Two of them, Martin Van deMark of Cut Bank and Forrest Werts of Great Falls had been in college elsewhere and were notable for their efforts.

That first year Freshmen leaders introduced their own publication, *The Prickly Pear*, providing an excellent window on Wesleyan life and accomplishments. In their view:

> The college department of the school this year has been one of interest. The future success of Wesleyan depends upon the materializing of a college department. At present the first two years of college work is being offered and the class this year, while not the largest in the school, has been one of the most active. The greater events of the year have centered around the college men and out from the present infancy of the collegiate department shall come one of the strongest colleges in the State. To the students who have finished their academic or high school work the University offers a department in college work leading to the Degree of B.A. and B.S.[5]

Adams remembered those first Wesleyan Freshmen with an evident fondness, some names familiar to Rocky Mountain College administrators many years later, persons prominent in the Methodist ministry, a well-known physician in the Midwest, a young man from Belt who became a pioneer in institutional development work. They valued their time at Wesleyan and contributed significantly to its progress. When nature's decree finally ended their school in Helena, they remained interested in its successor on the banks of the Yellowstone. They came to Billings for reunions, one to receive an honorary degree, another to be enrolled in the Rocky Mountain College Alumni Hall of Fame, another to help the college in its development program. They were among those who never questioned whether Wesleyan was worthwhile, for they were among those who knew it best.

Yet, time was running out for the Helena school as an academy with a grade department. High schools were penetrating the rural scene, in the smaller towns and villages, while business schools were growing in the cities and there was talk of technical institutes and junior colleges. The need remained for an open door to learning for youth from the farms and ranches, but that was the same population to which the Polytechnic Institute in Billings was successfully appealing.

These and other concerns engaged Wesleyan trustees as they met in Helena on June 25, 1915 to reflect on the past quarter-century and plan for the future. Dr. Bovard had invited Edward Laird Mills, former board chair, to address the gathering and he used the occasion for some frank remarks:

> It cannot be made too plain that the deficits referred to have been natural, inherent and inevitable. If the trustees deserve censure at all it is because in their attempt to keep the deficits low, they have more than once run the school so cheaply that it was no credit to Methodism. There is a standard below which it must not be allowed to go—just where that standard is, is a debatable question. There is no doubt, however, that if the trustees had put the standard still lower and avoided all deficits, the school wouldn't have any friends left today.[6]

Mills preferred the continuation of the academy and one year of college until there were sufficient resources for a full collegiate course. Bovard and Adams, however, urged moving ahead and the trustees agreed. Yielding, too, to pressures from the denomination's University Senate, they set the goal for 1917, with the elimination of grade work in 1919 and the phasing out of the academy in 1923.

Meanwhile, the Klein campus was in dire need of some beautification. Helena Hall was a lonely sentinel of learning east of town, backgrounded by the capitol and Mount Helena, without benefit of pavement or lawn. Adams remembered that the "campus was barren of trees and the roads from Eleventh Avenue to the Sixth Ward wandered freely over it."[7] The task would take years, trying to make something of the clay soil. A start was made, however, with the planting of some trees around Helena Hall and the seeding of a lawn. Unfortunately, the water pipe from town was too small to serve all the varied needs of a growing institution.

President Bovard's last year in office saw continuing efforts for the endowment fund that yielded, however, minimum results. His frequent absences from the campus in pursuit of funds were noted in *The Prickly Pear* with some sadness, that "we have seen only a little of this big, jolly, cheerful gentleman."[8] He submitted his resignation that summer of 1916, declined the trustees' request to reconsider, and moved back to church work and to the Superintendency of the Butte District. That kept him close, and he was a frequent visitor at Helena Hall, utilizing his new capacity to garner Conference support for the school.

MONTANA WESLEYAN COLLEGE

Charles Bovard's departure left Paul M. Adams in charge, until a new president came in April of 1917. The dedicated and resourceful Adams proved his worth in administration as well as in the classroom. The latter, however, was his decided preference, and he declined consideration for the presidency. Meanwhile, it fell to him to guide the process towards full college status being urged by the denomination's University Senate. That body guarded the gate to accreditation and greater church support. It was requiring of the Montana school a full college curriculum, better academically trained teachers, a president who was more than a fund raiser, and a name change appropriate for the institution.

The last condition would be met at the Conference of 1917, authorizing the changing of the corporate name from Montana Wesleyan University to Montana Wesleyan College. For a new president, the trustees located another Mid-Westerner to head their school. Reverend Leon H. Sweetland was a native of Missouri, another farm boy who had worked his way through an education, with A.B. and M.A. degrees from Northwestern University. His studies at Garrett Biblical Institute won high recommendations, and he was brought to Helena from his pastorate at Maywood, a suburb of Chicago.

The personable new president lost little time getting acquainted. Leaving Adams in charge of daily operations, he pushed preparations for a full college curriculum, printed it in the fall catalogue, while also recruiting additional faculty to fill new positions. Adams remembered that the instructional staff for the fall of 1917 included one with a Ph.D., six with M.A.s, and three with B.A.s. "In addition there were numerous instructors and teacher's assistants. It was an exceedingly strong faculty in numbers, in scholastic preparation and in ability."[9]

Among the new arrivals was Allan C. Lemon, former Superintendent of Schools at Culbertson who had been sending students

The new Mills Hall on the Klein Campus officially opened October 30, 1919.

The Klein Campus, on Montana Avenue, was close to a mile from downtown Helena.

Allan Lemon was a versatile coach, teacher and administrator.

The Wesleyan Male Quartet and Glee Club helped to make the school well-known and increase its prestige around the state.

to Wesleyan. A graduate of Morningside College, with additional study at the University of Iowa, he combined responsibilities in History with coaching Athletics. Winning records in football and basketball (without a gymnasium) attested to his skill, strengths of character, and team spirit. *The Prickly Pear* for 1918 noted: "He was able to do for Wesleyan the very thing that was needed — the establishment of real athletics." The versatile Lemon also served as Dean and established a Department of Education.

Fred W. Kelser was another who made a notable difference in Wesleyan life. He had attended Otterbein College in Ohio and came in 1917 both to teach Vocal Music and to complete his senior year. His contagious warm ways bolstered student spirit, while his work with a male quartet and later the glee club made the school well-known in Methodist churches around the state and elsewhere. In Adams's view, to Kelser "must go much of the credit for the rapid advancement in enrollment and the increased prestige of the school both in Helena and the state at large."[10]

Among the old-timers, Mary Eva Foster was still at the school, teaching English, serving as Principal of the Academy, and contributing her poetry to *The Prickly Pear*. The issue for 1919 would note: "She hath done much for Wesleyan." Others mattered and peopled the memories of grateful Wesleyan graduates across the years. For a small school living on the margins of survival, it was fortunate in the quality of teachers who chose to be a part of its mission.

President Sweetland's arrival in the spring of 1917 coincided with America's entrance into World War I, impacting college enrollments across the land. Wesleyan had some volunteers and inductees from the faculty and student body but, surprisingly, that fall saw an attendance of 116, of whom 55 were boys and 61 girls. There were 35 registered in the liberal arts curriculum. *The Prickly Pear* for 1918 observed that it had been left with half its staff intact.

The major accomplishment of Sweetland's short stay would be the construction of a new Mills Hall on the Klein campus. The campaign for a girls' dormitory was approved at the Conference in Billings in late August of 1917. It came at a time when the National Church had launched a campaign to celebrate the centenary of Methodist missions, with a goal of $40,000,000 to be paid over a period of five years. Dr. John Hancher from the Methodist Board of Education was again in town to report that 19 million had been raised for 42 colleges and universities. He explained the details and supported President Sweetland in his presentations to the Conference.

Dr. Bovard was vocal in his support, moving that September 9 be designated as Wesleyan Sunday and the time to launch formally the Montana campaign. The action taken was not only to raise $50,000 for the dormitory but, as a larger goal, another $250,000 for endowment and needed equipment. Enheartened by advanced gifts and the response in a statewide campaign, trustees proceeded with construction plans, and the foundation for Mills Hall was laid in May of 1918.

Meanwhile, wartime conditions brought a unit of the Student Army Training Corps to Helena in 1918. Two companies were organized, one at Wesleyan and the other at Mount St. Charles (later Carroll College). Adams assumed responsibilities as one of two instructors involved with classes, housing concerns, and mess hall matters. Two of the cadets were advanced to Officer Training School. By mid-1918, Wesleyan had 19 faculty and students serving on the Western Front, including 4 lieutenants, 2 sergeants, and 1 corporal. Others would be in Europe before the war ended in November.

Commencement in 1918 saw the first graduates with baccalaureate degrees since 1901. The class numbered two, namely Martin Van deMark and Fred W. Kelser. Transferring from Dakota Wesleyan, Van deMark was one of those promising young students who entered Wesleyan in 1914 intent upon having a full college education. He was a major player in campus life, Editor-in-chief of *The Prickly Pear*, captain of the football team, member of the Wesleyan male quartet, along with participation in various clubs. He sat alone on the platform, for Kelser had been inducted but had been granted his diploma. Both men returned to Wesleyan, Kelser to teach Music and Van deMark as principal of the Academy.

Campus activities in the fall of 1918 were affected by the worldwide influenza epidemic. Football had been reintroduced the previous year, with a schedule cut short by an outbreak of scarlet fever. The only game played in 1917 with the Billings Polytechnic Institute resulted in a scoreless tie, but *The Prickly Pear* noted with satisfaction that for most of the game the ball was in Poly territory. The schedule for 1918 was limited to two in-town contests, one with the Academy and one with Mount St. Charles, both Wesleyan wins. Other sports for the boys included basketball, track, and tennis, while the girls had basketball and a drill team.

Aside from Athletics, Wesleyan did not lack for student organizations, including Y.M.C.A. and Y.W.C.A. groups, two literary clubs, student government, Dramatic Club, Forensics and Music activities. They required participation by the same small band of students, thus nurturing talent and leadership potential. Wesleyans fared well in competition with other schools, winning honors, for example, in state extemporaneous speaking contests, honing skills which would serve them well in the ministry or other professions.

In the classroom, a faculty of 15 kept contacts close and caring. President Sweetland valued those associations and added to his responsibilities teaching English, Philosophy, and Bible. Among the Helena students in 1919 was Frank James Cooper. He was not in the cast of "The Fortune Hunter" presented that year by the Dramatic Club; rather, *The Prickly Pear* would describe him as "an artist of no small ability." Later, he would be known as Gary Cooper, the famous movie star.

Students and trustees appreciated the new Wesleyan head. For the latter, he was:

> A Christian educator of the highest type, whose brief term of office so far has demonstrated a grasp on the details of the situation and a broad vision and program for the future which we are confident will soon place our school in the front ranks among the colleges of the state.[11]

The Methodist University Senate was sufficiently impressed with developments in the Helena school to grant Wesleyan provisional accreditation, followed later by the American Association of Colleges.

Grade level work was dropped in 1919, and the Academy was scheduled to be phased out over the next few years. Enrollment continued to grow, despite the hard times that came with the collapse of the Homestead frontier. Drought ended the hopes for an agricultural Eden in the high plains, while foreign markets dried up following the end of the war. Recession gripped the entire land, but persisted in Montana throughout the 1920s, when 60,000 discouraged farmers left the state. Montana was the only one in the nation to lose population during that decade.

Along with the economic adversities, President Sweetland faced significant cost overruns in the dormitory construction, due in part to labor problems and increases in materials. The new Mills Hall would call for far more than the estimated $50,000. An exhausted president, bordering on broken health, submitted his resignation twice in 1919 before it was accepted. The Conference's Board of Education reflected the feeling of many: "He has left in Montana an enduring monument in our new dormitory which will ever stand as substantial evidence of his successful labors."[12]

Professor Allan C. Lemon was named Acting President, moving from his teaching and coaching post. Reverend Charles M. Donaldson, minister at St. Paul's who had been assisting with the Centennial Campaign, was given charge of financial matters, especially completing the funding for the new dormitory. That proved to be a daunting assignment, requiring $40,000 in immediate money for the project and another $20,000 to settle remaining bonds on Helena Hall. New bonds were issued for $60,000, leaving some $35,000 of floating indebtedness. Mills Hall was formally opened for student occupancy on October 30, 1919. For his part, Donaldson was named president in 1920, with Lemon serving as Dean.

The passing scene at Wesleyan was nowhere more apparent than with the death of "Brother Van" in 1919. He was at the Annual Conference in Glendive, along with old friend Jacob Mills, optimistic as always, praying persuasively for the school he had known from its beginnings. Other causes had also claimed his energies and enduring dedication—the Deaconess School in the valley, Deaconess hospitals, the many churches he had founded. But education never ceased to matter for the unlettered preacher on the Montana frontier. He died that year on December 19, age 71, lowered flags at the state capitol tokening the loss of one whose life, even then, had assumed legendary proportions.

THE FINAL YEARS FOR WESLEYAN 🔅

President Donaldson's tenure saw a notable increase in attendance, with registrations reaching 216 by 1923. Of that number, 146 were enrolled in the college. According to plan, the Academy was being phased out with the elimination of the freshmen class. There were 16 full-time faculty, with a number of part-time instructors. Paul M. Adams' "settee" of subjects had been whittled down to a single post, that of teaching Biology, the subject in which he had taken his Master's Degree at Northwestern University. He still had little time for leisure, as his teaching load was one of the heaviest in the college.

Another teacher of enduring influence at Wesleyan and Intermountain Union College came in 1920. Gertrude B. Crane was a Helena native, attended one year at the university at Missoula, then served as a missionary in New Mexico. Following study at a Bible school in Chicago, she came to Wesleyan to teach Bible and English and to complete her senior year. Graduate work came later at Garrett Biblical Institute in Chicago, Northwestern University (M.A.) and Union Theological Seminary in New York City (M.A.). Adams remembered that Crane's classes in Religion and Philosophy were always crowded with students, that "perhaps no other teacher put the stamp of her personality on College and student groups more indelibly than she."[13] Gertrude B. Crane is among the honorees in the Rocky Mountain College Alumni Hall of Fame.

Mention of the Lemons and Cranes does not diminish the contributions of others who served the college long and well. Surviving graduates of the Wesleyan and Intermountain Union years will have memories of those shaping lives beyond the historian's ability to relate. Adams remembered that "intimate and pleasant" faculty associations compensated in part for meager salaries. Married couples and single teachers met at least once a month in homes, at the school, or sometimes at the Placer Hotel for an evening of entertainment. Even the "most staid" members were forced to unbend and an hilarious time was had by all.[14] Later, in a more serious vein, papers were read followed by discussions.

1922 Wesleyan Men's Glee Club

1922 Wesleyan football second team.

Student activities also crested, including winning seasons for the football team. Coach Lemon performed minor miracles with a limited squad. In 1922 the Wesleyan "Orange and Blue" took on all competition, except the university in Missoula which refused a game. The state college in Bozeman fell 16-0, Mount St. Charles (renamed Carroll College in 1932) 20-0, 28-6, while the Polytechnic in Billings was trampled 90-0. Only the Miners in Butte survived with a scoreless tie on a snowy, windswept field. A trip to Idaho produced victories over Gooding and the College of Idaho.

An energetic Allan Lemon also found time to coach Forensics teams that fared well in the state and traveled afield to Washington and east to colleges in the mid-west. Wesleyan's little group gained the attention of the national Forensics society and membership followed in Pi Kappa Delta, the first chapter in Montana (1920). Another Lemon initiative was the School of Journalism with its bi-weekly paper, *The Collegian*. Work on the four page publication led several graduates into prominence in the newspaper field.

Music was another activity in which the little school had an influence disproportionate to its size. Fred Kelser, or "Kels" as he was affectionately known, had started with a male quartet before the war, but upon his return from military service soon had a glee club in the making. It became a selective organization, where membership was deemed an honor. The big event of the year was the glee club's concert held in the Shrine Auditorium with 3,000 people in attendance. There were also extended trips throughout the region, plus numerous appearances in churches. "Kels" moved easily in Helena society and its business community and was a real asset to the school.

The Glee Club's appearances also served recruitment purposes. The late Marion Cravath Van deMark Arnsberg remembered a train ride in 1921 from Sidney to enroll at the Polytechnic in Billings. That was her family's school, which her sister and other relatives had attended. On board with the usual farmers, ranchers and their families were members of the Wesleyan Glee Club, which had just performed at the Sidney Methodist Church. They were noisy, high-spirited, sharing jokes, stories, and songs which were not the ranch girl's particular "cup of tea."

Then one of their number, older and a leader, asked to sit with her, to avoid the soot and cinders sifting in through his window. Soon the conversation centered on the virtues of the Helena school, known for its teachers and scholarly ways, he said, and she agreed to stay over for that evening's concert in Glendive. Marion was impressed and the Poly lost out as she not only enrolled that fall in Helena but later became her train companion's wife, Mrs. Martin Van deMark.

In appreciation of the faculty and addressing a critical need, the Board approved in 1920 an increase in salaries, amounting to nearly $7,000, bringing the average pay to $1,605. Fortunately for the budget, The Methodist Board of Education provided special gifts of $7,500 for both Wesleyan and Gooding College in Idaho. That helped the school weather another season of financial stringency. It also enforced the recognition that Wesleyan had to become fully accredited to receive the Methodist Board's support reserved for well-established colleges. President Donaldson would report to the Conference Meeting at Miles City in August, 1921 that Wesleyan's education program had been certified by the State Department of Education. The next goal would need to be accreditation by the North Central Association of Schools and Colleges, with endowment remaining a major hurdle.

Donaldson noted that a School for Rural Pastors would be opened in the fall, as a part of the college's plans for greater usefulness. It would last for two weeks and would be staffed by "an able corps of instructors." He expected that the program would enroll a hundred pastors from Montana and Dakota Conferences. This and other developments led Supt. Bovard to sound a positive note at the gathering in the old cowboy capitol.

> Its full complement of College classes, including a fine graduating class, the largest valid enrollment, the fine Esprit de corps in the faculty and among the students, the numerous intercollegiate victories where both brain and brawn were in competition, have given our school an academic standing that it has not previously enjoyed.[15]

Bovard's confidence in Wesleyan's prospects seemed to be confirmed by developments in the 1921–22 academic year. Despite continuing drought and financial depression, the college enjoyed both its largest Freshman Class (42) and number of graduates (13) in a total enrollment of 103. In addition, 19 students completed work in the Academy. Campus improvements included doubling the size of the lawn, a new athletic field, tennis courts, and expanded sidewalks, all adding greatly to the general appearance.[16]

The next year witnessed an even more dramatic growth, with 64 students in the entering class in a total enrollment of over 200 for the year. There was talk of a new building, new equipment, and additions to the faculty. The *Montana Wesleyan College Announcement* for January, 1923 listed a number of new course offerings spread across the liberal arts curriculum. The School for Pastors had been postponed but was rescheduled for May, 1923.

The North Montana Conference with the Montana Conference had proclaimed February 4, 1923 as Wesleyan Day, when all the Methodist pastors were encouraged "to present the case of Christian Education and the claim of Montana Wesleyan." Generous offerings were stressed, while "a ringing appeal may direct some young life to Wesleyan" and "interest some man of means to give aid."[17]

So it was a season of hope, still troubled, however, by continuing financial pressures. They hung like threatening storm clouds over Mount Helena. Weary trustees had exercised every economy without severely damaging the school's standing. Still, each year's operations yielded deficits, adding to an accumulated indebtedness of over $95,000, including bond obligations. Conference support through the eight per cent sustenation program was shifted to the Centennial Fund, with money coming back to Wesleyan from the Methodist Board of Education. That amounted to over $12,700 in 1922 in a current operations budget of $37,000 and included a grant plus student loans and scholarships for returning veterans.

Like his predecessors, President Donaldson returned time and again to the importance of an adequate endowment as the answer to financial health. "From whatever angle one may view the affairs of Wesleyan," he told the Conference in 1920, "the necessity of an endowment is seen to be imperative."[18] Further, he noted the requirement of the Northcentral Association of Schools and Colleges of a $400,000 endowment for accreditation. Despite hard times, he urged all friends of Wesleyan to "gird ourselves" to raise such an endowment and turn the tide of financial fortune.

Biology class.

Home Economics class.

Philodorian Literary Society, Montana Wesleyan College, 1917.

Meanwhile, something had to be done to meet pressing needs. The Methodist Board of Education again provided leadership for campaigns in those sections of the state where there seemed to be a chance of success. The southwestern portion, including Great Falls and Lewistown, was canvassed and produced nearly $20,000 in pledges and collections. Another campaign centering in Helena raised over $46,000 in cash and subscriptions. President Donaldson and Wesleyan leaders were encouraged by this latest effort, but it was still another stopgap endeavor in what seemed like a long twilight struggle to keep the college open. Even the more optimistic felt a growing weariness with the task.

The vision had been for a denominational school, Montana Methodism's response to the westward spread of Wesleyan institutions. Time, however, was running out on heroic measures in economizing and dependence on Methodist resources alone. Survival in some form required involvement by at least another church body, and Wesleyan and Conference leaders now turned their attention to that possibility. It became a priority for President Donaldson, until his resignation in April of 1923, by which time merger negotiations with the Presbyterians' national board were nearing a conclusion.

Edward Laird Mills was among those favoring union with another school or two. He had served on the Wesleyan Board for many years, seven as president. There had been, in his view, the memorable moments, such as the move to the Klein Campus with the erection of Helena and Mills Halls. But there also had been no escape from the ever-present debt, requiring trustees from time to time to sign personal notes at the bank. Methodist laity, in sufficient numbers, had never really "owned" the school, supporting it adequately or sending their children to it, leaving it too much to faculty and preachers to be the sacrificial givers.

From his position on the national Methodist Board of Education, Mills questioned the wisdom of the church's policy of continuing to plant colleges across the West in the face of the growing secularization of American society. The Board, he noted, (*Plains, Peaks and Pioneers*, 116–19) still thought that Christian colleges "could be started in the happy-go-lucky fashion characteristic of the mid-nineteenth century." Some starts had been reconsidered, but too many, such as Gooding

College in Idaho, were doomed to failure. In a sense, then, the Montana Methodists were also the victims of a "nationwide unenlightenment." But if the Helena school had been launched on an ebb-tide, the proposed Intermountain, in Mills' view, could develop under firmer and happier auspices. Success would be more sure with three or more churches involved.

THE ROAD TO UNION ✖

The times generally were favorable for interdenominational planning and action, modeled by the Federal Council of Churches and exemplified by the Home Missions Council uniting 23 church bodies in common endeavors around the country. Montana had its own state Council by July of 1919.[19] The connection with colleges seemed obvious and led to several proposals.

Interestingly, one came from the Presbyterians, not content with the Deer Lodge venture being the final word. Rather, in July of 1921 at its Annual Meeting in Great Falls, the Synod received and adopted a recommendation to establish "A Union Christian College For Montana:"

> That the Synod of Montana hereby propose to the citizens of Great Falls and to the Baptist denomination, to the Evangelical Association, United Brethren, Christian Association and to any other Evangelical Christian denomination, that we undertake a start for a college within five years.[20]

Such an endeavor should include provisions for a campus with at least 40 acres, three buildings, a library of 5,000 volumes, a "standard" liberal arts curriculum, competent faculty, and a minimum of $500,000 in endowment. For their part, Presbyterians would contribute the remaining assets of the College of Montana and commit to $300,000 over the five-year period. Great Falls would be expected to donate a like amount in land, buildings and cash. The Baptists would be responsible for another $300,000, with any other selected denominations giving what they could.

With a membership in 1921 of nearly 8,000 in 96 churches and six Presbyteries, the Presbyterians were clearly major players in any plan for church-related higher education in the state. But they fared no better than the Congregationalists in trying to locate a college in the Electric City.[21] Rather, the following March they received an invitation from the Methodists "to cooperate with us in building up and maintaining a college of liberal arts at Helena."[22] That offer came from a meeting of national and state Methodist leaders in Spokane, Washington on March 9, 1922. Butte District Superintendent Bovard and President Donaldson were in attendance.

Interest built in a union college at another meeting the following month, April 11, 1922, when nearly 50 state and national denominational officials met in Helena and gave "considerable attention" to the matter. Two proposals were discussed and left dangling, namely, that the several Protestant church bodies unite in support of the Polytechnic Institute in Billings or that Wesleyan be designated the union college with the Polytechnic as a "First class academy," both institutions under the same governing board. Obviously with the latter, the tradition of a four-year classical curriculum weighed heavily in their discussions.

Meanwhile, Reverend Newman H. Burdick, minister of the Helena Presbyterian church, had been present at the Spokane gathering and was designated to carry the Methodist invitation to the next meeting of the Montana Synod. He was well positioned as a member of the Synod's Relocation Committee (charged with studying merger possibilities) and was personally committed to seeing the union with Wesleyan come about. Gertrude Crane was a prominent member of his congregation and Professor Chadwick played the organ. In addition, a number of the college students attended services. Burdick would have a major role in the negotiations that followed.

No final action was taken at the Synod's Annual Meeting in Missoula on July 12–17, 1922, but a Joint Committee with the Methodists was established to develop a plan of merger. That plan would provide for a holding corporation for the new institution and for the continuation of the governing boards of the merging colleges. They were to exist for 10 years to protect assets in the event that the merger should be dissolved. The College of Montana had assets and cash of $54,651.43, while Wesleyan properties and other assets were appraised at $281,474 with liabilities of $105,702. The new governing board was to have 13 members, 4 from the Methodist Conferences, 4 from the Synod, and 5 chosen at large by the board's church members.[23]

Union talk was also stirring interest beyond church circles, with the Helena business community expressing support. The *Montana Record-Herald* for January 12, 1923 carried the Commercial Club's strong endorsement. "Consolidation of Montana Wesleyan with the Presbyterian denomination has been actively pushed by the Commercial Club. Our special committee has attended several meetings, and assured the proponents of this move that when the time comes for such action Helena will do her part. This would mean much to the city in an educational way and would bring about an enlargement of this university."

The Synod on July 5–12, 1923 voted general approval for a "Plan of Merger," with further details to be worked out by the Joint Committee. That document was to be presented to the Presbyterian General Board of Education and then returned to an adjourned Synod meeting for final action. Methodist members of the Joint Committee had been granted power to act by their denomination. The Committee's task was accomplished at another meeting in Helena on August 31st and Reverend Burdick, merger plan in hand, was dispatched to New York City.

The Methodists were in town at that time, listening to Governor Joseph M. Dixon applaud their Conference, making "particular mention of the merger between the Presbyterians and Methodists in the management of Montana Wesleyan College," finding it "commendable that two such religious institutions should unite in the building of a college, emanating Christian ideals for the good of the state.[24]

Presbyterian Board approval came in late September, with the following provisions:

1. That the moneys now held by the trustees of the College of Montana be used as endowment for the new institution, and that these same moneys shall be held by the trustees of the new college under the same conditions as they are now held.

2. That the details of the merger be referred to the Secretaries to reduce to writing, and then, and then only, to be effective.[25]

The latter provision was implemented in a "Five Party Agreement" between the three college boards and the two denominational boards, lengthy and technical in nature, which became the legal basis for the union.

Final action by the Presbyterians came at the adjourned Synod session in Helena on October 23rd. Interestingly, one of the more perplexing problems was naming the new institution. At least ten suggestions were advanced with an early preference for Westminster-Wesleyan College. But that seemed to close the door on possible participation by other denominations, particularly the Baptists. Also, a hyphenated name suggested something short of true union, too symbiotic for what was intended. Paul Adams remembered that it was preacher-author-trustee George Mecklenburg who came up with the happy solution of Intermountain Union College. So it appeared in the Articles of Incorporation filed on October 27, 1923.

TRANSITION TO INTERMOUNTAIN

It was understood that the new era would begin with the coming of the first Intermountain Union president, a Methodist by agreement. Until that happened in July of 1924, Dean Allan Lemon was once more in charge, having been appointed following Dr. Donaldson's resignation in April to return to the pastorate. Prospects were excellent for the year, with the largest enrollment yet expected to begin classes on September 13. New appointments added to faculty strength. A winning football team was in camp at Hauser Lake. The Glee Club had ambitious plans for tours in the region, while debaters were also expecting to travel afield. Merger talk, it seems, had only quickened the tempo of life at the Helena school.

Lemon was definitely upbeat in his remarks to the Conference, noting strides forward in his six years with Wesleyan, observing that "we have one of the best little colleges to be found anywhere in the country. We take off our hats to none of them when it comes to scholarship." The coach in him added: "For two years now we have been conceded by the sports writers of the state to have the best football team in the state." Also indicative of Wesleyan promise was the large number of students pursuing graduate studies in eastern universities, including several in theological seminaries.[26]

That fall of 1923 found a Freshman class of 65, the largest to date, in a total college enrollment of 146. There were 58 students in the Academy, along with several special attenders, bringing registrations to 216. Tuition in both the College and Academy was $40 per semester, while board and room was $32.50 per month, due in advance. Student aid included scholarships, loans, and work opportunities. In the self-help tradition of the "Open Door, " the *Annual Catalogue* for 1924–25 assured prospective students that any "person who is ambitious and willing to work need have no fear of failure to earn funds enough to pay his way through the year" (p.23).

Intermountain Union College, the *Catalogue* made plain, "is a place for men and women to work." There were plenty of opportunities for students to enjoy sports, clubs, other activities and amusements, "but their importance does not overshadow the main purpose for which the students attend the college, that of making real scholarly attainment." Thus, "the idler, the loafer, the indifferent and the insincere have no place here." Those of serious purpose would "soon come to love the college for its traditions, its spirit and its associations" (p. 8).

The long deferred dream of a liberal arts college, to stand with confidence beside other Wesleyan institutions, had become reality by the time of Intermountain Union's advent. The school's academic program now provided for degrees of Bachelor of Arts, Science, and Music. Ten instructional departments offered courses in Biology, Business Administration, Chemistry, Education and Psychology, English Composition and Literature, Foreign Languages (French, German, Spanish, Greek, and Latin), History, Political Science, Sociology, Home Economics, Mathematics and Physics, Philosophy and Religion.

There were pre-professional programs in Law, Engineering, Medicine, and Theology. The curriculum was endorsed and subject to supervision by the two denominations' Boards of Christian Education. Teacher training work was reviewed by the State Board of Education. The College had membership in the Association of American Colleges, while the Academy was accredited by the Northwestern Association of Secondary Schools and Colleges.

The Wesleyan legacy remained in campus life, placing emphasis upon participation in school activities as an essential part of education for complete living. Aside from sports, there were various clubs, literary societies, opportunities for hikes and picnics, banquets and concerts, whatever and wherever the social enthusiasm of the school found expression. It might be a Glee Club performance with Professor Kelser at the podium, or at that football encounter of October 27, 1923 when a large crowd braved a cold westerly wind to watch their orange and blue clad "Panthers" hold mighty Brigham Young University to a scoreless tie.[27]

The big "W" on Mount Ascension would yield to an "IU," but otherwise the school below changed little in spirit and orientations. It was firmly Christian in purpose and program but not sectarian, "reverent but not dogmatic." It drew students from several denominations and sent graduates to seminary to fill their pulpits. It was both the privilege and duty of the Christian college to stress the moral and religious dimensions of education, not only through stated exercises (chapels) but in the nurturing environment of class room and campus life. The teacher's role was ever critical:

> The teacher imparts character more by what he is than what he says. It is personality that educates; it is character that begets character. Conscious of these deeper and more potent influences in the lives of young people, the College seeks to maintain a Christian atmosphere of the true and noble type in the class room, in the laboratory, and on the athletic field and campus.[28]

On the financial side, there seemed to be room for hope that union would improve chances for a more secure operation. The *Plan of Merger* provided for $10,000 annually from the two denominations and the proposed mounting in Helena of a campaign for $120,000. The Commercial Club had given assurances of its strong support. It was encouraging, too, that inquiries had been received from the Rockefeller Foundation concerning the new institution.[29] Among other possibilities, the door remained open to other denominations to join and add support. The moment, then, seemed to be one of promise but also of clear responsibilities. The *Plan of Merger* concluded with words of caution:

> Between the present and that ardently desired future there is a long, dusty road. Only two churches, as yet, are under the burden. If ever Intermountain is to come to the fullness of expectation, it will only be because both of these denominations, avoiding all mistrust and cherishing in each other complete faith and confidence, shall be willing to assume their responsibilities, and to make large sacrifices. Thus, and thus only, can the success of this great possibility be assured.[30]

Edward J. Klemme was the first president of Intermountain Union College, 1924–29.

President Wendell S. Brooks tenure, 1930–33 finally saw accreditation for the college.

Student life was obviously more than studying. It included various campus activities like this tug-of-war.

Chapter Six
Intermountain Union College

" The founders of Intermountain were men of vision; the teachers
of Intermountain are men and women of high ideals."
— *The Bulletin, Nov. 1931*

*The naming of Intermountain's first president revived an earlier
pattern of leadership* from the West Coast with Messrs. Tower, Van
Scoy, and Tenney. In keeping with the *Plan of Merger*, Dr. Edward J.
Klemme was a Methodist from Bellingham, Washington, a prominent
lecturer, writer, and educator. His degrees included an A.M. from
Northwestern University, along with graduate study at Stanford and
Columbia. In fact, he was enrolled in the latter institution when he
accepted the Intermountain offer, arriving at Helena in July of 1924.

He brought to his presidency a passion for teaching, urging at the
outset that the faculty "have faith in our task for it is the greatest in
the world."[1] Allan Lemon had added some promising new members
to an instructional staff of 14 with academic degrees and five instructors. They were mostly of the Methodist persuasion, but that would
shift over the next five years to a Presbyterian majority. Meanwhile,
Klemme found an institution with 148 enrolled in college courses
and 58 in the Academy. School spirit was high and the new president
received a warm welcome both on campus and in the community.

In September, he had the opportunity to meet all the Methodist
pastors, on the occasion of another long-sought consummation. Since
1908 the North Montana Conference had functioned as a separate

jurisdiction, reflecting the great distances, having equal representation in statewide planning, including the founding of Intermountain. Paul Adams remembered that each conference met separately in the old school in the Valley, then moved as one body to Helena Hall for business and, later, to St. Paul's Church for evening worship and celebration.[2] It was a good time for Dr. Klemme to make acquaintances and stir support among those grown weary with the school's long struggle.

THE KLEMME YEARS

Such support was no less needed due to the union; rather, Intermountain opened burdened with considerable indebtedness. That situation figured in merger planning, with a proposal to conduct a campaign in the fall of 1924 for $120,000. It would be held in the Helena area and called for Presbyterian leadership. The next year, the Methodists would be responsible for a drive focused on endowment needs. The campaign in 1924 produced enough gifts to reduce total college indebtedness to $42,000.

For the Methodists, an old friend returned the following year to engineer an endowment effort for $350,000. Dr. John Hancher of the Education Board required $40,000 for campaign expenses, money borrowed from a bank, secured by notes signed by faculty and friends. Nearly $300,000 was committed in cash and pledges, to be paid over a three-year period, the last due in October, 1929. The result seemed reassuring, but some subscriptions were canceled later, other payments postponed, so only $102,000 had been received by May of 1928. The endowment for that year was listed at $160,000.[3]

Clearly, it was not the best of times for fragile institutions like Intermountain to seek significant infusions of money. The state's mainly dormant economy was showing some improvement in the late 1920s and agriculture, still the anchor, was benefiting from better moisture. But Montana generally was outside looking in upon the blooming prosperity of the decade. The state lost population, the only one in the nation to do so. Financial institutions, greatly reduced in number, were recovering from the collapse of the Homestead Frontier. So there was more of caution in the air and less of that optimism that had characterized the earlier period.

While the financial outlook remained worrisome, the new president saw a future for Intermountain in establishing a Summer School. A cautious governing board, however, was unwilling to commit slim resources to a risky venture, and it became solely a faculty enterprise. The college did provide for advertising, while income from fees was divided among participating teachers. The first year, Paul Adams and four colleagues ventured with classes and were well rewarded for their two months of labor. That convinced others to join and the Summer Session became a regular offering, attracting not only students from Intermountain but state schools and some teachers. Later, visiting professors were added from such colleges as Carleton.

It was during Dr. Klemme's tenure that the Academy was discontinued, with the last class graduating in 1927. Paul M. Adams noted the end of an era with a tribute to 37 years of service:

> The Academy had served its purpose well...Its teachers had furnished inspiration and help to a multitude of boys and girls. The spiritual atmosphere had changed their lives and given them deeper visions of God and of Christian service...What it meant to the students can only be estimated. The fact remains that those who attended it, though many of them are now past middle life, still look back...to their teachers and comrades of that time and recall the name of Montana Wesleyan with affection.[4]

Among those whose lives linked the Academy with later Rocky Mountain College was Gertrude Rathbun Byfield Martin, Class of 1912. Rocky graduates of the 1950s and early 1960s will remember her as the ever-helpful, motherly manager in the Registrar's Office.

Jacob Mills' passing in October, 1925 was another end of an era happening. The resolute Vermonter combined business acumen with a passion for ministry, from the time of his arrival on the Montana frontier in 1882 bestowing over $170,000 on various institutions, including $67,000 for the college. Beyond money, his sturdy Christian faith, interest in youth, and willingness to serve had been a good match for Wesleyan's needs in its earlier years. "The passing of Dr. Jacob Mills," President Klemme observed, "a pioneer of pioneers, made every Montanan realize that he had lost a friend." *The Prickly Pear* for 1926 was dedicated to him.

Fred Kelser, esteemed
choral director.

Gertrude Boyd Crane was a
beloved teacher of religion at
Intermountain Union College.

Girls who earn a letter in the "I" Club must hike many miles,
play basketball, tennis, baseball and make a record in track.

President Klemme also took an interest in campus improvement. Under his direction, cement walks replaced the cinder ones from the streetcar line on Sanders Street to the college. Streets were paved and the city installed water mains. Black soil was brought from the neighboring mountains for new lawns, and more trees were planted. Perhaps his most valuable contribution was the extension of the campus to the west. Lots lying in two blocks each side of Tenth Avenue and between Roberts and Sanders were acquired at tax sales.

The college's athletic program, especially basketball, was severely handicapped by the lack of a gymnasium. The "Panthers" had to depend upon the high school facilities, but that was a poor substitute for having their own home court. It was reflected in losing seasons, despite student enthusiasm for the team. President Klemme, though not a strong supporter of athletics, sought a solution in a reduced facility within the college's financial means and obtained trustee approval to raise funds.

A *Supplement* to *The Bulletin* for November, 1927 sounded the motto "A new gymnasium for 1928," carried plans for the proposed structure, and added an appeal to donors: "If ever in your most gracious moments you have whispered to your soul a purpose to do something for Intermountain Union College, now is the opportunity to make it count" (p. 3). Not surprisingly, the Methodist clergy were the first to respond with their "widow's mite," pledging in all $2,500. Other subscriptions and cash donations added only another $2,500, perhaps reflecting existing commitments to the Helena Campaign and additional requests. Klemme figured on at least $10,000, including student and volunteer labor, so the project was deferred to a later day.

Meanwhile, each year saw growth in the newly merged college, largely, however, from the Wesleyan side. Methodist youth comprised more than half of the student body in 1926 (111), with Presbyterians (39) and Congregationalists (13) trailing well behind, along with a scattering of Lutherans, Episcopalians, Christian, Christian Science, Baptist, and no preference.[5] It was President Klemme's view that Intermountain had as large a student body as could be accommodated by the existing buildings and equipment. Helena Hall was the obvious example, crowded to the doors, serving various purposes, administration, classrooms, chapel—even the place for recreation and games.

Intermountain Union College's 1925 track team.

Intermountain Union College's 1926 girl's basketball team.

Methodists also led in faculty members (6), followed by the Presbyterians (4), Episcopal (3), Lutheran (2), Christian (1), Congregational (1), and no preference (1). Thirteen had M.A. degrees or had done graduate work. Missing were two stalwarts who had established places hard to fill by a mere closing of the ranks. Allan Lemon was granted a leave of absence in 1927 to pursue doctoral studies, following which he became dean of the College of Puget Sound and then head of the Education Department at the University of Idaho. Fred Kelser had resigned the previous year to return to Ohio where an elderly parent needed his care. Both men had been a part of the vitality Wesleyan had brought to the merger.

Paul M. Adams remembered other changes among his colleagues, including the coming of new faculty who added strength to the institution.[6] Among his students, he recalled Lauren Donaldson from Minnesota, nephew of President Donaldson, who majored in Biology and then took graduate work at the University of Washington. There he pursued a distinguished career in the Department of Fisheries, with research that won him a national reputation. The Donaldsons of Wesleyan and Intermountain days filled other places of leadership in community life and beyond, indicative of good tutelage at the little Helena school.

The Klemme years also saw regional accreditation for Intermountain as a Junior College. There was a change from the semester to quarter system, more money for student loans, and a business approach to budgeting that helped with financial concerns. The president felt good about the school in his report to the trustees in November, 1926:

> From the very first I have become interested in Intermountain Union College, not so much because of its present achievements, but because of its future possibilities. There is only one Protestant College with a full college course in Montana and Wyoming, and if there is a place on the planet where real service may be rendered, it is here....If it can be proven that we are in dead earnest regarding this College, and if it can be further proven that we are actually going forward, we shall have friends arising that we know not of.[7]

For whatever reason, perhaps grown weary with the financial uncertainties, Edward Klemme chose not to be a part of that future. He resigned in 1929 to return to Bellingham. His tenure had really mattered in those first years for Intermountain, building upon the heritages of the two schools, raising scholastic standards, moving beyond the Academy days, strengthening the Summer School, adding to the endowment ($156,236), still way short of accreditation standards for a college of 200 students, generally instilling a sense of confidence in Intermountain's future.

The *Prickly Pear* for 1927 put it well in dedicating that issue to Dr. Klemme– "to one who in three short years has proved his loyalty to our school, whose unfailing wisdom has stood the school in good stead many times when the success of the institution hung in the balance ... to a man among men."

STUDENT LIFE ❈

Wesleyan traditions remained to shape an enjoyable life at Intermountain. The first week of school brought the Annual Broadwater Party at the elaborate hotel and natatorium which C.A. Broadwater had built west of town. Freshman got dunked in keeping with custom by zealous sophomores and the year was off and running. More decorous behavior characterized the Y.M.C.A. and Y.W.C.A. receptions that first week and the Faculty Reception when formal attire was required. Some traditions yield slowly to changing times, for the formal President's reception was still being held at Rocky Mountain College in the 1960s.

Another ritual of the opening weeks was the party on Mt. Helena, at a large cave capable of accommodating an enthusiastic group of students. On one occasion, however, it became a bit crowded when a sudden snowstorm forced occupancy for an additional hour or two. Young spirits were undaunted by such emergencies which only reinforced the tradition. Fall also brought the annual freshman-sophomore football scrap with the winners hoisting their banner on the school's flagpole.

The big "I" on Mt. Ascension required attention twice in the academic year, with the Freshman assigned the painting task in the fall. In late spring, on Memorial Day, the entire student body picnicked at the location, applied new paint, and remembered Wesleyan comrades lost in the war. Headstones for the "I" contained their names.

Two big occasions capped the year, namely, "Sneak Day" and "Campus Day." The first, it seems, was a rather spontaneous affair, triggered by winter's release on the land, with evidences of spring at hand. Overflowing with pep, students abandoned the classrooms for more carefree places, preferably the Broadwater Natatorium. The privileged seniors added their own "Sneak Day."

"Campus Day" ranked as among the most important of the Wesleyan traditions, when everyone joined in cleaning, repairing, generally making the little school shine. Playtime was not neglected, with a "Frosh-Soph" tug-of-war followed in the evening by an "All-Intermountain Banquet" with prizes for the best decorated tables. Classes vied with each other in putting on "stunts." So, along with the regular activities of clubs and athletics, the *Prickly Pear* did not lack for events to include in the annual publication.

Aside from special occasions, daily life at Intermountain bore the heavy imprint of *in loco parentis*. Faculty and staff were dutiful in their roles, mentors of behavior as well as in academics, intent upon fostering a family atmosphere on the little campus. The girls in Mills Hall checked out and in, with 9:00 P.M. the rule on weeknights and midnight on Saturdays. Rooms were routinely inspected for tidiness, with the unwary risking grounding for infractions. Residents also learned early the importance of cooperation, since the dormitory had only one bathroom on each floor and limited laundry facilities.[8]

Meals were another time for family fare, with a student host and hostess presiding over a table of eight. Diners came in and left together and were encouraged to practice good manners. Many girls worked in the dining hall or found employment in homes. Lacking their own dormitory, many boys worked at odd jobs in exchange for rooms in private residences. So the tradition of the "Open Door" for youth willing to work continued at Intermountain, as it did later at the school in Billings.

WENDELL S. BROOKS AND ACCREDITATION ❖

By agreement the next president was to be Presbyterian and Dr. Wendel Stanton Brooks was selected. An experienced educator with nearly a quarter-century of teaching at secondary and higher education levels, he was a Yale graduate with an M.A. from the University of Chicago and a doctorate from Northwestern. He was currently on the Wheaton College faculty, outside Chicago, serving in the Education Department. Brooks had authored numerous articles in his field and also been a visiting professor at Cornell and the Universities of Michigan and Colorado. Thus he came with impressive credentials to Intermountain Union.

Interestingly, at Yale the versatile Brooks had combined scholarship with a lively interest in basketball, playing for the university team. In fact, he became a student of the game, later coaching a championship team in Connecticut and continuing to officiate whenever the opportunity afforded. Thus he became a strong promoter for a home court for the "Panthers." When an anonymous $10,000 gift advanced the possibilities for a new gymnasium, Brooks contacted a former colleague at Northwestern as to how available resources could best be used.

While at Wheaton, he had declined two offers for college presidencies and had not sought the opening in Montana. His obligations extended through the first semester and he did not arrive in Helena until February, 1930. Dean Henry W. Bruehl, another Northwestern product (B.A., M.A.), provided leadership during an interim which witnessed the collapse of the stock market in late October, 1929 and the onset of the Great Depression. Another season of drought added to Montana's woes, with the price for agricultural products hitting new lows. Once more, new leadership for the Helena school would be sorely tested by economic adversities of unprecedented proportions.

Despite daunting times, the mood at Intermountain was one of anticipation, awaiting the arrival of the new president. Hopefully, his contacts back East and in the Mid-West would benefit the college. Meanwhile, Dean Bruehl stressed the strong points of the Helena school—an able faculty, the "atmosphere of the college," and the quality educational product. In his report to the Board of Trustees on

October 22, 1929, he found encouraging trends in enrollment, reversing losses in recent years. Too, he had never been in charge of a more dedicated faculty. Very importantly, two Intermountain graduates were among 120 students accepted at Northwestern Medical School out of about 1,500 applicants.[9]

It cost the college, the trustees were informed, $320 yearly to educate a student. Since the average tuition, if fully paid, was $120, that left $200 per student to be raised. For Board Secretary David J. Donnan, that not only called for "PRAYER and PERSEVERANCE" but "lifting the level" of giving for all concerned. It meant people paying up overdue pledges or making new ones, the business community acknowledging what the school meant to Helena in economic terms, alumni more fully supporting their college, and two affiliated denominations reviewing their commitments to Intermountain.[10] Dr. Brooks wrote to Dean Bruehl that he was hearing good things about the college, its reputation, alumni accomplishments, ending with the "good work already done is just a challenge to us newcomers to do even better."[11]

The new president did have contacts around Chicago and elsewhere which he hoped to cultivate for endowment, buildings, and current operations. Those hopes faded as the Depression deepened, though he was able to salvage some $19,000 in new gifts during his tenure. It was badly needed as the college was entering a period when credit became more tenuous with Helena merchants. Fortunately, Brooks could count on C.H. Cruttenden, banker turned business manager, to minimize the damage. The even-tempered, kindly Presbyterian was a healing presence, while personally contributing financially to the ailing institution. Dr. Brooks must have pined at times for the relative calm of his Wheaton classroom.

Faculty salaries also fell victim to the Depression. Paul Adams remembered that for the first time in the school's financially troubled history pay rolls were not met. That was hard enough, but he later lamented that dedicated faculty were told not to complain, for there was a multitude of jobless Ph.D.s eager to take their places.[12] While few of his colleagues may have had any place to go, their willingness

English class at IUC.

The library was in the basement at IUC.

to somehow survive in their work belongs with the best in Wesleyan-Intermountain traditions. Eventually, they received about 50 cents on the dollar in accumulated salaries.

High on President Brooks' agenda was securing full accreditation from the Northwest Association of Schools and Colleges. That required a faculty fully equipped with master's and doctor's degrees. It also involved physical plant expansion for classrooms, a library, and laboratories. Thirdly, there must be an adequate endowment. Fortunately, new appointments had improved faculty academic credentials, though mainly at the master's level. Money, too, had been found to increase the library to 20,000 volumes and to employ a full-time librarian. The need for more physical plant involved reviving the gymnasium project.

President Klemme had left $5,187 for that purpose in a building fund, to which an anonymous donor added $10,000 in 1931. Dr. Brooks was gladdened by an opportunity to signal progress amidst hard times, to provide employment for students, and to address accreditation requirements. The new gymnasium would have a full basement with classroom and laboratory facilities. The main floor would have a full sized basketball court and a stage with dressing rooms for dramatic and other performances. Ground was broken in 1932 and cornerstone ceremonies were held in December. Work progressed slowly, but enough was accomplished to hold commencement in the unfinished structure in 1933.

Meanwhile, the endowment picture had brightened in 1929. The assets of the College of Montana had been retained by the Presbyterian Board until certain debts of the institution had been repaid to it. Intermountain received the interest but could not claim the principal until all financial matters were settled. That happened in 1929, raising the endowment to nearly $250,000. The Northwest Association sent a representative to Helena in 1933, whose favorable report resulted in a full four-years' accreditation. A long road had been traveled from that first feeble effort at higher learning out in the Prickly Pear Valley.

Enrollment fell but not drastically due to the hard times. It averaged over 200 students during the Brooks years, with a low of 175 in 1930 and a high of 237 in 1932. *The Prickly Pear* of 1933 reflected leaner times with fewer pages and advertisers, cheaper paper, less handsome covers. In a foreword, the editors explained that it had been a year "fraught with many difficulties and struggles...(yet) days of happiness" (p. 2). Games were still played, the Glee Club still entertained appreciative audiences around the state, debaters somehow still made it to events throughout the Northwest and further afield. Despite the Depression, affectionate notes to teachers and classmates scribbled on *Prickly Pears* in the College Archives attest to years well spent.

Campus life in the 1930s saw some changes in activities, with the old style literary societies giving way to new clubs centered around various departments: Biology, Chemistry, Drama (the Black Masque), English, German, and History. The *Circle Francaise* was for students in the Romance Languages and put on an elaborate entertainment, the *Soiree*, each spring. That was also the season for the all-school banquet when four young ladies were elected queens of their classes and one young man reigned as the Student Prince. Their pictures, of course, adorned the next *Prickly Pear*.

No campus, then or since, is without some student concerns and for Intermountain one focused on prohibitions of dancing and card playing. In 1920 the General Conference of the Methodist Church had relaxed rules against such amusements, but the Montana churches were slow to follow. The merger with the Presbyterians was viewed by students as a hopeful development, but it was not until 1933 that the issue was resolved. President Brooks argued that the campus was a far more desirable place for dancing than Helena's numerous night-clubs and the trustees finally agreed.

Dr. Brooks saw in the achievement of accreditation his principal accomplishment, one which moved Intermountain into a new day. He reminded the faculty of what it meant to join ranks as an equal partner with the colleges and universities of the Northwest. He wrote in the *Prickly Pear* for 1934:

> This new accrediting places upon the Trustees a new responsibility for the financial standing of the College, a new responsibility on the Teachers for its scholastic standing, a new responsibility on the Students for the tone, the life, of our campus. With this one aim now achieved, let us work happily together for the maintenance of this ideal and toward the accomplishment of still other worthwhile aims.

Brooks had relocated rather frequently in his career, with the four years in Helena among his longer stays. Interestingly, his next move was to Billings, to help the Polytechnic Institute establish a liberal arts curriculum. That lasted over a year, followed by another college post, then a longer tenure as Superintendent of the Chicago Tract Society. His final years were spent in the Congregational ministry in Michigan. He died in 1961.

The departure of yet another president caused Paul Adams to reflect upon that remaining continuity in leadership which steadied the little college in its pursuit of "worthwhile aims." No one equaled his own tenure reaching back to 1905, but there were others such as Gertrude Crane, inspiring students since 1920, William Wible in Mathematics since 1922, and Elise Sicher in French and Spanish since 1923.

Wible also served as Dean and could report in an article in *The Independent Record*, April 24, 1932 that the year had been a good one for Intermountain Union. The Depression, then bottoming out, added to the usual financial strains and stresses, but among the accomplishments, the debate team had swept Montana colleges in a string of ten victories and gone on to compete successfully in national intercollegiate contests at Tulsa, Oklahoma. The French Club, under Elise Sicher's watchful eye, had held its second annual *Soiree* at the Placer Hotel, which *The Record* characterized as "one of the most successful entertainments of the winter season."

In these and other ways, Intermountain Union colleagues had seen their school gain in Helena's confidence, drawing many more students from the local high school and an occasional transfer from the Catholic institution. Methodists continued to outnumber Presbyterians two to one in the student body, but there were now more of the latter on the faculty. The Academy was a valued memory. Campus life reflected an older and more mature student body. Despite the continuing hard times, the ongoing battle of the budget, Intermountain was a college finally come of age.

Faculty log homes were designed by President Bunch and located a block west of campus.

Rev. Jesse Bunch was the last president at Intermountain Union College

The new gym at Intermountain Union College before the earthquake of 1935.

A deputation team was organized to lead worship services in surrounding churches on weekends. They would present various musical selections, read scriptures and give personal witness of their own Christian lives and faith.

REVEREND JESSE BUNCH ❖

Intermountain Union's third and final president was the Director of the School of Religion and campus pastor at the State University in Missoula. Another graduate of Northwestern University and Garrett Biblical Institute in Evanston, Illinois, Jesse Bunch had come to the Montana Methodist Conference in 1915, first serving parishes in Fort Benton and Roundup. He was known for his interest in youth, promoting and adding a gymnasium to one of his churches, providing energetic leadership in the Conference's work with young people. A doer by nature, he moved on to the District Superintendency head-quartered in Helena.

It was there he became deeply interested in Montana Wesleyan. Along with good friends such as Martin Van deMark and Vernon Lewis, he became involved in the merger movement which led to Intermountain Union College. Characteristically, he was among those urging President Klemme to move ahead with the gymnasium project. When his time came, it was his great pleasure to see that long-deferred dream brought to fruition—only to fall victim to nature's capricious decree.

Jesse Bunch's friendly personality and happy ways made for a welcome if brief stay. He was not unacquainted with the sobering task awaiting him, including a floating indebtedness of nearly $20,000, an unpaid faculty, and bonds of $40,000 due in two more years.[13] Problems of a more intangible nature included growing weariness of both denominational officials and clergy in support of the school. Interest engendered by the merger was waning. Some ministers opposed the new policy permitting dancing, though as Adams noted, they did little to confront the pastime in their own congregations.[14]

Then, too, Methodist and Presbyterian youth had the option of attending other church-affiliated colleges in Washington and the Dakotas. The state added to competition with the establishment of Northern Montana College in Havre and Eastern Montana Normal College in Billings. Northern, in particular, invaded Intermountain territory, which drew many students from communities along the Great Northern Railroad. So keen competition added to problems of institutional viability.

The "Swan" cast, 1931, was one of many theatre productions at IUC.

The Men's Glee Club of 1931.

Intermountain faculty and students during the year of 1935–36 in Great Falls. Photo includes a nursing class from the hospital.

Adjustments were made with faculty and merchants, freeing the president to take up the challenge of the unfinished gymnasium. That remained for him a high priority. Working with the determination of a Nehemiah reconstructing the walls of ancient Jerusalem, he busied himself raising additional funding, obtained donated materials, persuaded the students to assess themselves at $5.10 each, and also contribute to the project in lieu of publishing another *Prickly Pear*. He issued a call for volunteer labor, resulting in clergy and laity from around the state coming to the campus for two weeks. It was a gratifying response and resulted in a completed facility ready for winter basketball practice. That season saw a return to winning ways for the Panthers.

The second major project engaging President Bunch's energies was started in the summer of 1935. Reverend Edward Smith, veteran preacher in the Conference and District Superintendent, had donated lots north of Sanders Street suitable for a housing project. The plan was to construct four duplex log structures to be used as residences for faculty and the president at nominal rentals. Construction began but was interrupted by the earthquakes in October. Completed in the spring of 1936, the log homes proved to be a good source of income for the school relocated in Billings.

THE HINGE OF FATE

Winston Churchill's title, "The Hinge of Fate," for Volume IV of his history of World War II comes to mind in what happened next in the Wesleyan-Intermountain story. He explained its choice in connection with the reversal of Allied fortunes, determining the outcome of that great struggle. In the case of the college, it was an act of nature that finally quelled an irrepressible will to survive in the pursuit of church-related higher education. What drought and depression among other adverse conditions could not accomplish several earthquakes in October, 1935 did bring to pass. The little school in Helena was forced to close.

Earth tremors were not unknown in the capitol city, with an occasional episode as a reminder of the area's vulnerability. On June 27, 1925 an earthquake of sizable proportions centered in the Gallatin Valley was felt in Helena. So it was no cause for great alarm when on

October 4, 1935 the ground trembled and rumbled and windows rattled. One week later, however, early in the morning there was a more serious quake, toppling dishes from shelves and cracking plaster in Mills Hall. Old-timers were not that concerned, but the newer arrivals felt a mounting anxiety.[15]

Another week passed and found the Intermountain Panthers playing football at the School of Mines in Butte. It was a close contest with the Helena team prevailing. Victory felt especially good, since the Miners had won in recent years. So there was a big celebration back home that evening in the new gymnasium. A group of enthusiasts climbed Mt. Ascension to illumine the big "I." Just as that happened, several severe tremors shook the building, the floor swayed, the lights went out, and a section of wall collapsed inward, narrowly missing seated students. There was no panic as the celebrators retreated to the lawn—more disbelief of what was happening.

Mills Hall also suffered considerable damage, leaving students to grab bedding and spend that night on the lawn. Some slept from exhaustion, but most were too excited or cold as cars streamed by along Eleventh Avenue. Fearful residents were seeking the presumed safety of the countryside.

Daylight revealed extensive damage to campus buildings. The plaster was down in all rooms in Mills Hall and there were wide cracks in the brick facing of exterior walls. Helena Hall fared even worse, with the concrete frame sprung and some interior walls in ruins. It was declared unsafe for occupancy, but Mills Hall could still be used with repairs and cleaning.

There was extensive damage to buildings throughout Helena, with city authorities closing schools and forbidding public meetings for one week. On the campus, the college's cook had joined the flight from town, prompting a number of resourceful girls to organize a kitchen staff. Breakfast was available cafeteria style not long after the regular hour. Many students returned home to await developments, but those who remained arranged social events to find in friendship something of comfort in a tragic hour.

President Bunch gathered the faculty for what had to be the most unusual meeting in the history of the school. They met on the lawn, grateful for a warm, sunny day in late autumn. He did not minimize the problems as he asked for their cooperation in seeing what could be done to carry on. Gertrude Crane remembered that both old-timers and the newer teachers vowed unanimously to stand by their school, with or without salary, whatever it took to keep their college in operation.

The students were close behind in pledging their loyalty to Intermountain. They joined in a cleanup effort, removing tons of plaster from Mills Hall, repairing and renovating where possible, walking the mile to the Presbyterian Church where classrooms had been arranged. That became a real test of determination with the arrival of subzero temperatures. Mills Hall was made habitable and the crippled institution labored on with remarkable grit and devotion.

But it was all to no avail, for on Friday, October 31, a seemingly vindictive nature returned in relentless fury, though somewhat less on the Richter Scale than the earlier earthquake. It lasted longer, however, and came in two waves, pretty much finishing Helena Hall. To remain would mean to build up from the foundations, an insurmountable task for even the most devoted. Besides that, there was a strong desire to salvage the year, if at all possible. With that in mind, the Board adopted the suggestion of a member from Great Falls to relocate in that city.

Amazingly, the November hegira to the Electric City was accomplished within one week. Trucks were made available with volunteer drivers to transport beds, bureaus, other dormitory possessions, dishes, books, laboratory equipment. The girls were to occupy the fourth floor of the Deaconess Hospital, while classroom facilities were available at the Methodist Church. The boys bunked in the basement. The Baptist Church allowed the use of its kitchen and dining hall for the boarding students. Equally amazingly, 138 of the 157 students made the transfer to Great Falls, with some local enrollees making it 166. It was a makeshift affair, but Adams reckoned that the year was concluded satisfactorily.

As a matter of fact, it was the first year since 1915 that the college enjoyed a balanced budget. That was a source of satisfaction for a beleaguered president who had been given the terms for continued support by the two denominations. There would have to be a physical plant worth $300,000 with expansion to $500,000 within ten years.

For the same period, the current operations budget would have to grow from $35,000 to $70,000 a year. In addition, there would need to be an endowment of $500,000. A weary, nerve-wracked Bunch was willing to try, but the odds were overwhelming.

The Helena campus was a gaunt shell, mocking the dreams and endeavors over the years. Hopes for relocation in Great Falls were met with some support but greater indifference. The Park Hotel near Gibson Park was available at a reasonable price and had the space both for dormitory purposes on the upper floors and classrooms on the lower ones. An architect was employed to prepare plans for alterations and a committee of local citizens formed for a fund raising campaign. It had the support of some prominent leaders, including the school superintendent.

Great Falls, however, already had a junior college for girls established by the Roman Catholic Diocese of Eastern Montana in 1932. There was strong support for developing the school into a four-year institution, which happened in 1939. Without assurance of the necessary financial backing, the Intermountain board voted to abandon plans for Great Falls and to close the school. It was a painful time as faculty went their separate ways, some of whom had been colleagues for many years. Students scattered to different institutions, regretting the loss of what might have been.

Then in August, 1936 President Ernest Eaton of the Billings Polytechnic Institute proposed a plan of affiliation with Intermountain which was acceptable. The college would maintain its autonomy, have its own governing board, while utilizing Polytechnic facilities. The move was made for the fall quarter, but few students remained to relocate to Billings.

Professor George H. Gloege, Intermountain graduate who returned to handle Chemistry and Physics, was the only faculty member to move, spending three years on the Poly campus and a longer tenure at Eastern Montana College. An heroic President Jesse Bunch left that fall for Pacific Grove, Oregon and a far less stressful pastorate in that college community. Later, his name would be placed on a little chapel within the Paul M. Adams Memorial Library at Rocky Mountain College.

Intermountain brought to Billings its regional accreditation and classical curriculum. Reverend Joseph Pennepacker moved from back

East to become Dean of the College of Liberal Arts and to care for Intermountain's interests. Baccalaureate degrees were granted by "Polytechnic-Intermountain." Back in Helena, enough securities were sold to cancel $42,000 of remaining bonded indebtedness. Later the Montana Deaconess School acquired the Klein Campus, paying $30,000 for Mills Hall and another $5,000 for the other two buildings.

REFLECTIONS

It was less than half a century from beginning to ending, this courageous venture in church-related higher learning. For many of the years, Methodists had to settle for remedial and secondary training, with pretentious titles for the school a matter of hope for the future. The setting was hardly auspicious in a sparsely populated state, subject to a sluggish economy whose mineral wealth tended to go elsewhere, with other private and public institutions vying for available students. The school's backers were mostly clergy and laity of the rank and file, without the powerful leadership to command sufficient resources. So Wesleyan and Intermountain were seldom, if ever, free from financial difficulties.

They did not lack for loyal friends, such as the Fred Gamers and Richard Lockeys early on, the Brother Vans giving sacrificially from slender salaries, and others who responded to repeated appeals which mostly fell short of their goals. But Jacob Mills stood alone as a major benefactor. Methodists generally were not known for their wealth, but there were others of material substance who could have joined him had the little school stirred their interest. Following the merger, there was a Presbyterian layman or two well-established in the financial community.

It is notable, too, that all of the institution's presidents but two were clergymen, dedicated but not strong in administration and fund raising experience. Paul Adams concluded that in spite of the good work all of them did, none was able to make the college an outstanding institution.[16] To be sure, that also required a strong governing board, able to open doors of opportunity for the cultivation of substantial contributions.

The veteran teacher was quick to point out that despite the limitations the school was on the upgrade and had good prospects at the time the earthquakes came. The value of Intermountain's work was recognized by other educational institutions in the state, notably its leadership as a church-related college. A main focus all along had been on the development of character, more intangible in measurement but an abiding influence for good in the lives of the many who had studied at the little school.

That included approximately 400-degree graduates. They were well prepared as some pursued advanced study at leading universities, others careers including teaching, ministry, law, nursing, and business. Wesleyan and Intermountain graduates were well regarded as teachers, while others served the church as pastors, and in the missions field, not only in the Methodist fold. Further testimony to good tutelage was the notable number of second-generation enrollees at the College.

In any reflection on the Wesleyan years, one turns again to those youth who came, many with rudimentary schooling, some in the need of discipline, to learn from teachers who shared their faith and kindness, stirring within their young charges an interest in knowledge. Something of that venture with fledgling minds and spirits, mining potential, must have been in view that day when two veteran teachers stood pondering the earthquakes' devastation, weighing the investment of all their years. Had it been worth it? What of roads not taken? There was really no question, they agreed, for what mattered most was not bricks and mortar, even the end of dreams, but the opportunity they had had to share in the unfolding of young lives, the worth of which defied the knowing.

Further reflection on the Wesleyan and Intermountain Union years comes to rest upon one life which, more than any other, spanned the years and personified what the school sought to achieve. Paul Milford Adams was the "beloved Prof," revered by students, esteemed by colleagues, another legend in his own time in Montana Methodism. In grateful recognition, Intermountain Union conferred upon him an honorary doctorate in Science at the June commencement in 1930.

Following the College's closing, Adams continued to teach at the Deaconess Hospital Nursing School in Great Falls, retiring in 1943. Then came supply preaching and the writing of a book, *When Wagon Trails Were Dim*, published in 1957. Earlier on November 8, 1949,

150 former students, colleagues, and friends gathered for an appreciation dinner at the First Methodist Church in Great Falls. Letters poured in from distant places, too many to read, with messages of affection deeply felt. But perhaps the best testament to "Prof" was the placing of his name on the new library at Rocky Mountain College. That happened in 1959, the same year he died at age 85.

There are those for whom the Wesleyan and Intermountain stories do not end—as long as memory survives. For the years do not dampen the affection for a professor or diminish friendships made long ago. In a way, it was the kind of drama a Greek writer of tragedy might have devised, an Aeschylus or a Sophocles, all the dreaming, caring, enduring, finally with a new gymnasium as a seeming symbol of vindication—only to be crippled beyond hope by capricious fate. But what survives are the intangibles of the human spirit, including the sounds of distant voices echoing across the years.

Service of Silence, held at the beginning and end of the school year on the Rims, 1914.

PART THREE

BILLINGS POLYTECHNIC INSTITUTE

Beginnings
The Uncertain Years
The Way to Union

Aerial view of the Billings Polytechnic Institute in the 1920s.

Chapter Seven Beginnings

" You know that the beginning is the most important part of
any work"
— Plato, *Republic*

*Their vision called for a location with sufficient land for a good
farm and room to provide training in the various industries of the
region.* That had not been available in Deer Lodge, along with the
opportunity to shape policy for their kind of institution. In search
for a new setting, Lewis and Ernest Eaton looked eastward, to Billings on the Yellowstone as more the center of a vast inland area.

The brothers rode over to the "Magic City" in early June of 1908,
to explore the possibilities of starting a school. They visited first with
Ignatius D. O'Donnell, prominent citizen and well known for his
pioneering work in agriculture and irrigation farming. Upon learning
the Eatons' intent, he took them to see John D. Losekamp, another maker
of Billings, known for his interest in promoting education for youth.

In fact, the portly merchant had been concerned for years in starting
the kind of school the Eatons had in mind. While others dreamed of
personal wealth on the frontier, this farsighted citizen worried about
the many young people in the more remote places in need of the
education he had missed. He knew about polytechnic schools elsewhere and believed that approach to be the most appropriate for this
part of the West. O'Donnell later remembered that as he introduced

the brothers and their mission, Losekamp peered over his glasses and exclaimed: "Boys, you are just the fellows I'm looking for." That was when the Polytechnic story began.*

BILLINGS 1908 🔯

John Losekamp was not wealthy, but his business had prospered and surely there were others to join in such a good cause. His town was booming and an obvious location for an institution meeting the educational needs of the region. The population had more than doubled since 1900, now approaching 10,000 residents. Proud citizens could boast new schools and handsome churches, a hospital, the Parmly Billings Memorial Library, and an Opera House featuring the best of entertainment by traveling road companies. Prosperous times were evident in the new Northern Hotel boasting "the finest cafe in the Northwest," general business expansion, six banks, and the construction of a large sugar factory.

On the civic side, there was a new city hall and fire station and a new county courthouse. Not lacking were able leaders in the prime of life, to become the merchants, staff the counting rooms, and fill the ranks of the various professions, including public office. An early account reckoned that Billings had more "farseeing, enterprising (leaders) that usually fell to the lot of towns along the line."[1] From all appearances, then, it was the kind of progressive city that appealed to the brothers from Maine.

Losekamp was certain that Billings was bound to prosper, and with it an institution seeking to train youth off the outlying farms and ranches, the small towns and villages and declining mining camps. With high schools 100 miles and more apart, many would be limited to an 8th grade education, if that, and so deprived of the opportunity for further learning leading to productive livelihoods. That situation haunted the Eatons and the Losekamps, stirring strong convictions about the work to be done.

---

* Ignatius D. O'Donnell papers, Harley O'Donnell Collection. This indicates that both brothers came to Billings, while a *Gazette* account refers to one "well known educator in town."

John Losekamp's time with the Billings Polytechnic Institute would be cut short with his death in 1913, but it is doubtful that the school would have survived its infancy without his determination to keep it open. Born in Ohio in 1850 of immigrant German parents, his family had moved to Kansas in 1854, the same year that the ill-fated Kansas-Nebraska Bill unleashed violent sectional passions that moved the nation closer to the abyss of civil war. Gold discoveries in the Black hills prompted a move there in 1877 to provide a boot and shoes business for the miners. Then news of the Northern Pacific Railroad's penetration into Montana led to the family's wagoning over in 1882 to the tent town of Billings, counting upon the Magic City to live up to its name.

A young enterprising Losekamp took over the family store, expanding its line of western wear, soon building a prosperous trade in its location across from the new Parmly Billings Memorial library. But he was more than a merchant, plunging into the civic affairs of his town and territory, serving on the city council, as acting mayor, in the legislature, after statehood promoting a bill for county free high schools. He was also an ardent sportsman, enjoying field and stream, importing a flock of Chinese pheasants to see if they would adapt to prairie life, stocking Beartooth Mountain lakes with a variety of trout from back East, seeking legislation to promote the wildlife of the state. It is notable that his bequest to the Polytechnic included four race horses!

John Losekamp's openhearted generosity became legend in the city, at Christmas inviting boys and girls to his store for the annual gift of dolls and toys. But it was the Polytechnic that was closest to his heart, beginning with a $10,000 contribution and then his ongoing support, including the word around town that he personally would be responsible for unpaid Poly bills, even if it meant selling his store! Indeed, there is no accounting of the Institute's beginnings without a due remembrance of this man who really made a difference.

POLYTECHNIC FOUNDED

It was on June 11, 1908 that *The Billings Daily Gazette* reported that some "principal men of the city" were discussing the establishment of a polytechnic school. They had been in contact with an unnamed

Ignatius D. O'Donnell was a prominent Billings businessman and one of the founders of the Billings Polytechnic Institute.

John D. Losekamp was a Billings merchant, and founder and major Poly benefactor

Construction begins in August, 1913 on Kimball Hall, the first dormitory for women on the Polytechnic campus.

"well known educator" who viewed Billings as an ideal location for such an institution. Noting the popularity of such technical schools in the East, he predicted that the proposed Billings venture would easily enroll 1,000 students within a few years and in time would become "the largest institution of its kind in the northwest."

The *Gazette* article went on to note that the "educators most closely allied with the movement are particularly fitted to interest eastern men of wealth, as they have already raised a large sum for a similar school in a less promising locality than this." If they could find funding for endowment purposes in Deer Lodge, they should have even greater success securing support for a school in Billings.

Promoters of the proposed polytechnic institute were busy that month making contacts around town, meeting with such success in obtaining subscriptions to the "college fund" that they called for an organizational meeting for Friday, June 26. All citizens interested in higher education were invited to assemble in the city council chamber, at which time the visiting educators (the Eatons) and leaders would explain what needed to be done.

"It is hoped," *The Gazette* editorialized, "that all Billings boosters and every one interested in seeing a higher educational institution located here will attend the meeting." The paper had caught the spirit and had even grander visions for the endeavor at hand:

> The proposition to establish a higher educational institution in Billings should interest every resident of eastern Montana. Such an institution, if started now, would undoubtedly eventually develop into one of the great universities of the country.
>
> There is no university, taking the broader meaning of the word, in the state of Montana. Our lawyers, our doctors, our dentists, our professional men of all crafts, except pedagogy and engineering, are now educated outside of the state. It is time that Montana developed a real university. There is no place where one could be more rapidly developed than in Billings.[2]

So the proposal for a polytechnic stirred resentments that eastern Montana had been largely ignored in parceling out state institutions. As it happened, the meeting called for the 26th was postponed, due to the absence from town of several key promoters.

Dedicated educators, Lewis and Ernest Eaton, inspire Billings community leaders to support an institution of higher learning.

Kimball Hall.

It was rescheduled for the 29th. Banker Preston B. Moss chaired that meeting, held in the city council chambers, with merchant Henry White serving as secretary. Enthusiasm reigned in the crowded room when it was announced that seven men in the city had already committed $40,000 towards the needed $75,000.

John Losekamp had started the fund with a gift of $10,000. The Yegen brothers, Peter and Christian, pledged a similar amount. Moss, Ignatius D. O'Donnell, and canal builder Henry W. Rowley committed $5,000 each. Mayor William B. George added $2,500, with other subscribers including Russell Shepherd, Judge James R. Goss, Austin North, Mssrs. Hart and Albin, Albert L. Babcock, Henry White, Edgar Camp, A.C. Logan, and Dr. James Chapple. It was an impressive cross section of community leadership.

The occasion that evening stirred the usual speeches. Moss was certain that the moment was right. Losekamp spoke of the practical side of the institution, how it would help innumerable boys and girls and also bring industries and more prosperity to the region. It would become the city's greatest attraction. I.D. O'Donnell expressed his great faith in what was being undertaken and what it would mean for the area. He also foresaw considerable eastern financial support once the school was established. Others like Col. Rowley and Christian Yegen were confident that the time was right to go forward with the project.

Lewis and Ernest Eaton, the unnamed educators, next discussed in detail their hopes and plans for the school, doubtlessly further enthusing the meeting with the wisdom of founding the proposed polytechnic. Ever in support of efforts to promote his town, the heavyset William B. George then added his customary stirring speech. With attendance at two colleges and a university, the mayor was one of the best educated in the room. "After his talk," the *Gazette* reported, "no one could doubt the advisability of placing the school on a definite basis."[3] Sleep must have come late that night as the two brothers relived a most gratifying evening.

Plans were made for the completion of the fund drive. Moss appointed Losekamp, George, O'Donnell, Christian Yegen, Camp, and Judge Goss to supervise the effort. The Judge, another early arrival from New York, handled the incorporation papers, filing with the state on August 4, 1908. The 17 founders proceeded to elect a board of trustees, with Losekamp as president, Christian Yegen as vice president, Henry White as secretary, and Preston Moss as treasurer.

Next came the question of the school's location and a difference in preferences. The Yegens favored a site near the river, while the Eatons were interested in some land northwest of downtown, beyond what is now Pioneer Park. The majority of the board, however, opted for a location three miles northwest of the city, 60 acres of irrigated beet fields owned by John Grange. The price was right and Lewis and Ernest found at last their "field of dreams."

PRESCRIPTION FOR THE POLYTECHNIC

Lewis and Ernest had been living with their plans and were ready to detail them in the Institute's first *Bulletin* of September 1, 1908. They reflected the new thinking in educational circles on the importance of industrial and technical training. It fits the students, the publication explained, "for the practical duties and vocations of life in this region and at the same time give(s) them that true culture of heart and mind which comes only through a thorough, general education."[4]

Instruction was to be offered in several divisions, namely, Science and Liberal Arts requiring a high school diploma, Engineering with a diploma or equivalents, Commerce, Industrial Arts, Teacher's Training, Academic and Music, all with an 8th grade education. The Academy would be basic in providing preparatory work for the other departments. The *Bulletin* noted that the four year program would prepare students for any Eastern college or university. Those not meeting minimum grade requirements would be admitted as special students and assigned work suitable to their needs. Thus, there would be an "Open Door" for all youth of the region.

A program in agriculture, with a wide range of studies, was designed to serve students planning to return to the ranch or farm. The campus would be divided, with land allotted for gardens, orchards, and pastures to keep students employed during the summer months. That would also help with tuition, room, and board at $210 per year. Billings residents paid $25 per term for tuition or $70 for the three terms if paid in advance. Parents were advised to provide youth with some spending money, 50 cents to a dollar per week deemed sufficient!

In a booklet entitled *Personal Story of the Polytechnic*, Lewis Eaton referred to their endeavor as "A Practical Christian School." It was to be a place "where any boy or girl might come and receive a useful training for life." He continued:

> Courses were to be related to the industries of the region and no effort was to follow the traditional high school and college program. Instruction was to be planned to meet the need of the individual student....The influence of the school was to be strictly Christian, but nonsectarian. While distinctly evangelical, the denominational differences and creeds were to have no place in the life of the Institute.
>
> An opportunity was to be provided through various school industries for boys and girls without funds to earn their way through school by remunerative labor, thus giving the poor an equal chance with those more favored. Every day the student was to come in vital contact with the making and growing of things and classroom work was to be correlated with work in the shops. Actual work in all industries was to be a part of all training and a wholesome respect and love for all labor would be taught.
>
> In order to teach the student the responsibility of citizenship and inculcate the proper respect for law and order, the institute was to be organized as a model state where the students were to make and enforce the laws.
>
> In the course of time when the demand was evident, a high grade college was to cap the institute. The one supreme purpose of the Polytechnic was to be the development of an all-around useful Christian citizen, trained to take a place in the industrial, social, political, and religious life of the region.[5]

The emphasis upon a Christian school was a clear commitment for the Eaton brothers. It was part of their upbringing and what mattered greatly in the development of values and a mature outlook upon life. Lewis and wife Mary were Congregationalists, while the Ernest Eatons were Episcopalians. Both of those denominations claimed several members on the first board of trustees, along with those from other communions.

The founding of the Poly caught the interest of Rev. Gregory G. Powell, Superintendent of the Montana Congregational Conference. Headquartered in Billings, he noted in his *Diary* for June 22, 1908: "Called on some of the men including Mr. Eaton about the college movement in Billings and had talk with him 're: our getting behind it.'" That led to an action at a Missoula meeting of the Conference in October, 1909, endorsing the Institute as a "Christian school, in accord with Congregational principles and policies." Ties were strengthened the following March when Powell and visiting Dr. Hubert Herring, Secretary of the Congregational Home Missionary Society, organized a Polytechnic church, to be served by the local Congregational minister.[6]

IN PURSUIT OF IDEAS AND FUNDS

Congregationalists at the local, state, and national levels would provide support, though they were also interested in establishing in Montana a liberal arts institution. It was clear that the next move for the enterprising brothers was a trip back East to study similar institutions and to cultivate sources of support. They counted on previous contacts from their work in Deer Lodge to be of assistance. So, reassured by the beginnings in Billings, Lewis as Educational Director and Ernest as Financial Director spent several weeks that winter in Chicago and New York.

In the Windy City, they visited the Lewis and Armour Institutes. The stop at the latter provided an unexpected and gratifying response. Lewis wrote to Mary that the director there already knew about their work in Deer Lodge and the new venture in Billings. Conrad Kohrs, stockman-capitalist, benefactor of the College of Montana, was an acquaintance and had told the Armour's director "our whole history and said that we would build at Billings the greatest school in the west."[7]

Lewis felt that the time in Chicago had been productive, that they had "learned a lot of things" and appreciated the time both institutes had given to them. He was especially pleased that the Armour's dean had agreed to join the National Advisory Council they were organizing for their school. They also had a final interview with Dr. Daniel K. Pearsons, the philanthropist who had been the major supporter of the work in Deer Lodge. He remained interested in their endeavors, but no longer had the means to help. Lewis remembered his counsel:

> Billings is the best point in the country to build a great school. No region needs an institution more than Montana and Wyoming. You have the right plans for a school. My money is all gone, but you will find those to help you. You are sure to win.... Give the poor boys and girls a chance. Build good dormitories for them and give them a chance to earn their way. They will make the best of men and women.[8]

The Eatons' stay in New York City would lengthen into the spring. They soon took private rooms to live within the $1,000 provided by the Board of Trustees. An early contact, Gustav Stickley, editor of the *Craftsman Magazine* and furniture manufacturer, proved to be most helpful, leading to introductions to prominent New Yorkers. He was himself deeply interested in the proposed Billings school, agreeing to join the Institute's Council and traveling to Montana the next summer to help in the designing of the first buildings.

Stickley introduced the brothers to the Y.M.C.A.'s international secretary, who counseled them not to be timid in asking for support. New York philanthropists, he explained, were accustomed to large requests, for a million or so. He also noted that an approach to the Frederick Billings estate should be high on their list, that at the time of his death in 1890 it was worth an estimated 10 to 30 million dollars. It would seem that a sizable gift could be made to such a worthy cause, especially in the city that bore the railroad builder's name.

It was their plan to spend the first month meeting people, before preparing a prospectus and seeking commitments. Meanwhile, Lewis could write to Mary: "We never had such good prospects on an eastern trip. We are dined and feasted with the best."[9] Menus included boiled lobster, which Lewis allowed was "a little above our taste." Talk of large gifts also left the brothers rather breathless, increasingly excited by the seeming possibilities for the work in Billings.

Other contacts included Dr. Henry Prichett of the Carnegie Foundation, Dr. Clifton of the Congregational Educational Society, and Willis E. Lougee, treasurer of the Congregational Home Missionary Society. That last acquaintance would prove to be fateful for the Polytechnic, really justifying the Eaton's time and expense in their New

York stay. The native Vermonter would have the deep and enduring commitment that mattered greatly in the school's unfolding story.

By late February, the brothers had a prospectus ready for printing, containing 25 pages detailing their plans, with good illustrations, appropriate, they hoped, for a million dollar campaign. Time in the big city, the heady talk of large numbers, now stirred envisagements of a school for the entire Northwest, one featuring field lectures, correspondence courses, summer schools for teachers, ministers, and farmers. Lewis figured that it would take at least a million dollars, $600,000 for the college and $400,000 for endowment. He wrote to sister-in-law Emma Johnson: "I talk as if we had it. We shall get it but it may take a year."[10]

A side trip to Washington included a visit with the U.S. Commissioner of Education, who complimented the brothers on their plans in Billings. Montana's Congressional delegation, Senators Thomas Carter and Joseph Dixon and Representative Charles N. Pray were asked to support a request for $250,000 by the Carnegie Foundation. Its president, Dr. Henry Prichett, had encouraged the Eatons to submit a matching proposal. While in Washington, Lewis and Ernest also hoped to see the country's new president. That did not happen, but back in New York they joined in a mass prayer meeting for William Howard Taft.

FIELD OF DREAMS ▥

Letters from New York spoke of the need for continued contacts, but also for the urgency of returning to Billings and preparing for the opening of school that fall. Life in the big city was exciting, but Lewis confessed that he really preferred the quieter pace in Billings. He would return East next year with Mary for further fund raising, but it was clearly time to be at home and stake out the first buildings on their acreage west of town.

The Eatons had announced an opening date of October, 1909 in the region's newspapers, expecting to have facilities available at the new location. When it became apparent that this would not happen, space was rented throughout the town, including the basement of the public library, the second floor of Odd Fellows Hall, facilities at the Y.M.C.A., and John Losekamp's building. The Eatons obtained the old Fair Association exhibit hall (the "Octagon" still standing at North 25th St.) as a boarding house for boys. Girls were quartered in the Slayton residence on Yellowstone Avenue in the west end of town. In addition, Lewis had some cots for them in his home. That made for some walking through chilly winter mornings, but also a safe segregation of the sexes.

Classes were held in the basement of the library, Odd Fellows Hall, and the Losekamp building, which also contained school offices. Each morning at ten, students gathered for chapel or assembly at the Y.M.C.A. auditorium. Religion really mattered for the brothers from Maine, the nonsectarian type but firmly Christian, helpful too, they hoped, in heading off potential problems with student behavior.

Improvisation, then, was the order of the day, to cope with most trying circumstances. On October 9, 1909, however, the fledgling institution greeted nearly 100 students. They came from all over the "great neglected region" the Eatons sought to serve, from Montana, Wyoming, Idaho, and even Alberta. It was a territory, the brothers would observe in various publications over the years, greater than all of New England, New York, Pennsylvania, New Jersey, and Virginia combined. They would often draw a circle encompassing those states and more, noting the abundance of colleges and universities and another of comparable size in the Northwest with only a scattering of institutions.

Fortunately, the youth who came to Billings stayed despite all of the inconveniences, trusting, it seems, in the promise of this school of the open door. In fact, more arrived during that year, totalling over 150. One of their number was Clarence Holt, first to be enrolled and typical of not a few. He had ridden horseback from his mountain home at Lake View, Montana 125 miles to the nearest railroad station, sold his pony and traveled another 250 miles to reach the Magic City. He would not be disappointed with his years at the Polytechnic, remaining to ranch near Billings and later moving into town. At either place, the kindly Clarence never missed the celebration of the first candlelight supper on the new campus.

Work west of town involved clearing a beet field without benefit of adequate machinery, utilizing student labor, initiating their long involvement with school improvements, notably in the construction of campus buildings. First came a permanent structure, what is now Eaton Hall, for administration and classroom purposes. John Losekamp disliked brick buildings, preferring sandstone, but he deferred to the wishes of the other trustees. They would remember that in the later sandstone construction of Losekamp Hall. In addition, there were four frame bungalow dormitories, A.B.C.D. and a heating plant.

Unfortunately, winter came early that year, unrelenting with bitter cold and deep snow, complicating efforts to move to the new campus. Lewis remembered:

> We had to overcome what seemed to be insurmountable obstacles to carry out our purpose. It became necessary to dig water mains through frozen ground three miles from Billings to the new school buildings. On every side we could hear "It can't be done," but we said "It must be done," and with this one thing in mind we pushed onward although at times discouraged by the many delays that came.[11]

A break in the weather in late January, 1910 had brought warm winds from the West, melting the snow, leaving overburdened hay wagons to labor through miles of mud. It was about noon on the 31st when they started, one of the strangest processions in the story of American higher education, lacking none of the pioneer spirit that won the frontier, up 27th Street, then west along the Big Ditch, an ungraded way now called Rimrock Road, thence to the recently converted beet field.

It was a cloudy, dreary day, promising more of the same, yet powerless to dampen the spirits of faculty and students alike, headed at last towards their field of dreams. It was hardly an auspicious sight, the one building signaling something of permanence, the four temporary structures, connected by planks bridging ditches carrying heating pipes, and posing a problem for the unwary. The first arrivals found empty buildings, awaiting furniture later in the day. As wagons rolled in piled high with belongings, few faculty and students in that brave company of about 100 knew where anything was—a plight complicated by the gathering darkness.

They had counted upon having lights, but some thoughtless worker had neglected to complete electric connections. That, along with frozen water mains, contributed to rather primitive conditions for the first meal on campus. A hurried trip to town for candles solved the lighting problem. The dining room and kitchen occupied part of one of the bungalows, affording cramped space at best. Tables were plain, eating utensils in short supply, your choice of a knife or fork or spoon, a menu of sandwiches, warmed over potatoes, beans, and cocoa in a tin cup. Still, Clarence Holt recalled that they had a "jolly time."

He may have been one of the young men assigned the task of assembling the cots in the girls' dormitory. Temptation overtook them and the bolts were inserted just enough to hold the beds together but not to permit much movement. Consequently, cots were collapsing throughout the night, much to the dismay of the matron, Mrs. Valiton, leaving weary occupants on mattresses on the floor. Next morning, there were sly inquiries about how the girls had slept.[12]

The bungalows had central hallways piled high with trunks and other personal belongings, making for crowded quarters. Days passed in the former beet field as the fledgling venture in learning graduated from candles to lamps and finally to electric lights. It was, all in all, something of a miracle, appropriate for the Magic City. In a mere six months there was the beginning of a campus for a school housing 100 students, with more waiting to attend. As Lewis Eaton surveyed the scene, he may have remembered a conversation with Dr. Pritchard of the Carnegie Foundation, that the Eatons should keep things simple, offer learning for the common people, keep it within their reach, and begin with what you have.

The instructional task on the new campus was in good part a family affair, with Lewis as Educational Director adding History to his responsibilities, wife Mary handling Literature and Reading, Ernest as Financial Director teaching Economics, and Sister-in-Law Emma Johnson presiding over Normal Training and Industrial Work for girls. That had been her speciality in Deer Lodge. Other courses included Political Science, Mathematics and Engineering, Commerce, English, and Industrial Shop.

The Agricultural program soon gained in importance, with 40 acres devoted to farming and gardening. Produce was to be raised for

Willis Lougee was a
major patron and was
referred to as "Poly's Best
Friend, " and was named
honorary president.

Emma Johnson was a
long time teacher at
Montana College and the
Polytechnic.

*Student government of the second semester in 1914. Student training in government was
viewed as very important by the Eatons.*

the boarding department, to feed cows and horses, and for demonstration purposes. Later, the *Poly* for 1912 (p. 11) would boast that the Institute took 34 prizes at the Yellowstone County Fair and had exhibits at the Montana State Fair.

The first year was one for organizations at the fledgling institution. With notable purpose and energy, athletic teams were fielded, literary societies were established, the Polytechnic Church enrolled over 50 members, and a student government was put in place. It was, in fact, to function like the state government, with a constitution, legislature, executive, and courts. It mattered greatly to the Eatons that the students should have training for citizenship, with practical experience in making and enforcing laws. Political conventions on campus with elections and even inaugurations would be among the important events of the year.

Other occasions and observances which would soon become traditional included Moving Day (to the campus) or Anniversary Day, reenacting the Candlelight Supper. May Day celebrated ancient rites of Spring, finding students that first year gathered on the bank of a dry irrigation ditch, in the shade of the only tree on campus, erecting a Maypole. A King and Queen had been duly elected, who led the dance around the pole, students in Robin Hood attire after the old English custom. Then came games of strength and skill. As a later *Polygraph* remembered, students were in a mood "of rejoicing and carefree thanksgiving for the mere pleasure of being alive amid such bounteous opportunities."[13]

Commencement capped the year with May 27, 1910 finding five graduates on the platform. They had entered the school with advanced standing, one or more having transferred from Deer Lodge. Ceremonies included an address by Montana Governor Edwin L. Norris. Lewis Eaton reflected on the occasion with a note of reassurance: "We felt that we had demonstrated to all that there was an urgent demand for a school in this region and that the school could be built."[14] Further evidence of the need could be found in the growing number of students turned away for lack of room.

The *Polly* (changed to *Poly*) for 1910 observed that the "four months...the Polytechnic had occupied its permanent quarters have been full of pleasure and profit. Improvements are being made daily.

The first Polytechnic gymnasium was dedicated in 1912.

photo by K.F. Roahen

The engineering building, Tech Hall.

The Quarry was a source of sandstone for the Institute's buildings.

The Institute farm.

The grounds, which presented such rough appearance when the buildings were first erected, have been graded and seeded, and the whole place begins to take on a settled condition" (p. 6). I.D. O'Donnell would change the campus appearance dramatically, planting its first trees. When the Carolina poplars were winter killed, they were replaced by hardier varieties of ash, elm, and poplar, adding beauty along with shade on warm summer days.

GAIN AND LOSS

Unfortunately, that summer of 1910 brought a crisis in the city's banking institutions. Uncertainties lingered in the wake of the Panic of 1907 and the depression that followed. In addition, the economy felt the harsh winter of 1909–10 and drought that followed. The largest bank closed, with others also failing, jeopardizing more than 2.6 million in deposits. Subscriptions for the Polytechnic fell victim, leaving some $40,000 unpaid. Meanwhile, bills for the new campus mounted, and only the generosity of the school's main backers, principally John Losekamp, kept the doors open.

Big Eastern dollars also failed to materialize. Lewis had written home that he would be happy if they could raise $100,000 from their first visitation. In fact, by 1913 only $105,000 had been given by sources outside the state, and that included James J. Hill's $25,000. About 1,800 donors had given amounts ranging from $6,000 down to 50 cents.[15] Not all gifts were in dollars, as in the case of the Wyoming coal company that supplied the Institute with fuel for all one summer and well into the fall.

An otherwise bleak situation brightened with the prospect of a gift by the great railway builder. It was on March 17, 1911 that the Billings Board of Trade, John Losekamp, president, communicated with James J. Hill, supporting an Institute request for $25,000 to purchase 100 acres adjacent to the campus. The owners believed in the school and would sell below the market value. The Board "heartily endorsed" the use of the land for demonstration farms, noting the decided benefits for regional agriculture. The new Polytechnic, the Board observed, "is the only institution of its kind in the entire Northwest and the only school of higher learning in Eastern Montana, Northern Wyoming, and the Western Dakotas."[16]

Ernest Eaton's correspondence to St. Paul the next day laid out the full picture for the Institute's request, the school's aims, its beginnings, its current drive for $25,000, the importance of the land for its mission, a prospectus for the demonstration farms, along with a letter written earlier by Montana Governor Edwin L. Norris strongly endorsing the Billings venture. Eaton concluded:

> We ask you to come to the aid of the school in this way because we do not know where else to turn to save this land to the school and thus enable it to carry on its great purpose, and because we know you are strongly in sympathy with just this sort of education. We would be glad to give the demonstration tracts the permanent name of the James J. Hill Demonstration Farms, and extend to your agricultural experts whatever supervision you might desire over the work.[17]

Hill was no stranger to Billings and its environs, having attended a Dry Farming Congress there in 1909. The enterprising Empire Builder appreciated vision and initiative, saw the possibilities, and responded favorably later that year of 1911. It was indeed the kind of good news needed to enthuse the school's backers for further efforts in its behalf. The *Poly* for 1912 applauded the new land addition: "Its acquisition is invaluable... allowing the institution to carry out its broader plans and purposes, as it could not have done otherwise. The 160 acres now owned by the Institute will be the basis for the Model Farm School of America." (p. 11)

The early spring of 1912 brought an opportunity for Poly students to demonstrate appreciation for Hill's generosity. Encouraged by administration, they walked *en masse* from the campus to the railroad depot to greet him upon his arrival in Billings. It must have been one of the more warming responses he had received for his many gifts. The Institute also wasted no time that spring, planting crops and dividing the land for the model farm experiments the following year. Over 100 different vegetables and grain seeds were sown. Twenty acres were set aside for a dairy farm, with thoroughbred milch cows to supply boarding needs and provide produce for the market. Next came a 40 acre irrigation farm, to utilize the latest in crop rotation, tillage, fertilization, seed selection, irrigation, harvesting methods, all to help regional farmers.

Plans also called for a 20 acre fruit farm, with apple, plum, and cherry orchards. At least 10 acres would be needed for a seed farm, providing garden and farm seed, to be used at the Institute and distributed to area farmers. Other land was set aside for school gardens, a poultry plant, and a modern apiary. Finally, appropriate for the region, dry land farming techniques would be studied on the Great Northern Railway Demonstration Farm just north of the campus. It all made for an appealing layout in Institute publications, prompting the *Poly* for 1912 to predict that "scores of other schools will be patterned after it and its influence thus made world wide."(p.13).

Meanwhile, the Institute had acquired a gymnasium in late 1911 financed by the Billings Chamber of Commerce. The building was bare bones, just a plain, wooden frame structure, but destined to receive a sandstone facing with stones quarried from the Rimrocks. The new facility was a welcome accommodation for a "strenuous" schedule of basketball games. The gymnasium was dedicated on February 2, 1912, sharing that evening with Anniversary Day and another Candlelight Supper. Senator William B. George employed his usual eloquence in delivering the main address.

The graduating class of 1911 had more than doubled to 12, another sign of the need for more housing, enough, it was felt, to accommodate 300 youth. The Polytechnic's appeal remained the same and was reaching into the more remote places:

> This is the People's School, and any young person over fourteen years of age may enter. There are no entrance examinations, and diplomas from the eighth grade are not required. No matter how back in his studies the student may be, he will find at the Polytechnic work to meet his needs.[18]

For early student Clarence Holt, the first three years were ones of growth and development, and it was a joy to be a part of the beginnings. The various departments were now staffed by a faculty of twelve. The Music Program was blossoming with a Glee Club, Concert Choir, two quartets, and an orchestra. Campus organizations included a Christian Endeavor along with the several literary societies. The Polytechnic Church counted many members, while the student government was in full swing, presiding over the Polytechnic Republic, electing governors for each semester. In athletics, there was basketball (both sexes), football, baseball, tennis and track.

The Eatons continued to cultivate Eastern contacts, as well as issuing frequent appeals in the region. There were "Special Funds" for emergencies and campaigns to reach for major dollars. In addition to student fees and farm income, $10,000 or so was needed to balance the budget. Larger sums were required for dormitories and classroom facilities. And there was always the possibility of acquiring more adjacent land.

Ernest Eaton was back East for another extended visit in 1912, finding Willis Lougee willing to serve as Eastern Representative and thinking strongly about a complete involvement. His contacts with people of wealth, Russell Sage, John D. Rockefeller and others, seemed to promise great things for the Billings school. Another important contact was Amos L. Prescott of New York City. His initial gift of $50 paid for a load of coal, but his future generosity would result in Prescott Commons.

In reflecting on the Institute's beginnings, Lewis wrote that "no pen can describe the struggles of the past four years," coping with bank failures, faced with law suits, trying to locate money in the East, finding himself in Boston with only change in his pocket, experiencing, too, sickness and death "among our little band of workers."[19]

He may have been thinking especially of Jesse Belle Kirkpatrick of Chicago, recent graduate of Park College, enthused with the chance to teach English to youth on the frontier. She had only two years before illness had its way. But the books she loved and left, along with others given by her parents and faculty and students and others became the school's first library appropriately bearing her name.

Some other teachers, Lewis recalled, did not have Jesse's courage and abandoned the Institute at critical times. But there were also the triumphs and he thought particularly of the gift by James J. Hill which had broadened the horizons of their field of dreams. The farms were more than proving their value, winning the silver cup offered by the Great Northern for the best farm exhibit of 1912. "We have great visions of the future of the Polytechnic and believe that friends will be raised up who will make it possible for the school to extend its influence over this vast new country and bless the lives of thousands."[20]

In the midst of the struggles and triumphs, the Billings Polytechnic lost its best friend with the death of John D. Losekamp in August of 1913. The *Poly* that year had been dedicated to him (as was the first in 1908), to one "Whose Generosity, Linked with his Desire to Give the Young People of the Northwest a Practical Education, Has Made this School Possible." His bequest to the Institute that meant so much to him included $23,000 in cash, an interest in property in Billings and Wyoming, and some corporation stocks.

John Losekamp had spoken often of his interest in music as another way of fostering culture. He said on one occasion:

> I do not know of any greater thing I can do for the Northwest than to establish a conservatory of music where the young women of the Northwest can secure the very best advantages of a musical education. A great conservatory of music established in Billings will contribute much to refinement and growth of the coming generations.[21]

So plans were made for a conservatory, with the cornerstone laid in 1917 and occupancy in the spring of 1919. Appropriately, Losekamp Hall still graces the campus of Rocky Mountain College, and still houses a music program which is one of the proud traditions of the school. The visionary merchant lies in an unmarked grave in Mountview Cemetery, in the old section, close to where Central Avenue runs by. His real memorial, in addition to the building, is the difference he made in the lives of untold youth who entered the school of the open door.

The Losekamp conservatory.

Chapter Eight
The Uncertain Years

" Never look down to test the ground before taking your next
step: only he who keeps his eyes fixed on the far horizon will
find his right road."
— *Dag Hammarskjold, Markings*

*John Losekamp had the satisfaction of seeing a girl's dormitory under
construction, a much needed addition to campus accommodations.*
The frame bungalow had been intended as temporary housing for 20
students, but four years passed without a permanent replacement.
Early in 1913, a "strenuous campaign" was launched for funds,
yielding $1,000 after several weeks effort. That was deemed sufficient to
begin excavations, trusting in further gifts and student labor for much
of the construction. Stone would come from the school's quarry.

Word went out, and when the Polytechnic opened September 9,
1913, 42 girls were on hand to occupy the new facility. Unfortunately, it was unfinished, lacking a roof among other necessities. The
attractive stone and stucco building had been designed for 40 residents,
but in view of increased numbers, it was expanded to accommodate 60
students. That fall found girls crowded into the frame cottage, four
to a room, with trunks and other personal property piled high in the
narrow hallway. Here they lived, according to the *Polytechnic Bulletin*
(January, 1914) "in contented and happy expectancy for four months
waiting for the new home to be finished."

Donations came from 34 states and Canada, with the dormitory named for the major benefactor, Mrs. Flora Kimball of Portsmouth, New Hampshire. It cost over $15,000, about one half of what it would have been without benefit of student labor and stones from the quarry. The basement became home for the Domestic Science Department, properly equipped with all the appliances for a model kitchen. In addition, there was a dining room, sewing room, and a laundry. The first floor had rooms for 20 girls, music rooms, the parlor, and the matron's accommodations. The second and third floors housed the remaining residents.

Dedication services were held on February 1, 1914, with Dr. Hubert C. Herring as "honored guest" and principal speaker. It had been four years since the Congregational missionary leader had been on campus to help organize the Polytechnic Church. Lewis Eaton presided and was especially grateful that brother Ernest could attend. He was recovering from an extended physical breakdown. Still in his mid-thirties, the strains of Financial Director had required rest and recovery. It was a moment that really mattered in the life of the young school. The *Polytechnic Bulletin* (May, 1914) proudly observed: "It is safe to say that no institution in the West provides such a pleasant home for its girls as does the Polytechnic."

THE POLY'S GREATEST FRIEND

Occasions like Kimball Hall's dedication brightened an otherwise daily struggle to keep the Institute open. In addition to the building projects, some $10,000 in annual donations were needed to augment student fees and profits from farm produce. For Lewis Eaton, writing in 1913: "No pen can describe the struggle of the past four years at the Polytechnic; neither will space allow even a brief account of its hardships and triumphs."[1] For those bearing the heavy burden of raising money, it meant "sleepless nights and days of severest strain."[2]

Loyal Billings area backers stood with the Eatons, serving on the Polytechnic board, providing support, but it was an Eastern contact that helped to buoy their spirits during the uncertain years. They took comfort in Willis E. Lougee's deepening involvement, his willingness to serve as Eastern Representative of the Polytechnic. The well-connected Vermonter would play a vital role in the years ahead, similar to John Losekamp's in the early years. Lougee would be known as "Poly's Greatest Friend."[3]

The Institute's mission held great appeal for him. Its concern was with deprived youth, much like he had been, impoverished, growing up in rural Vermont, minimum schooling, with an ardent desire to make more of his life.

In his diary, *A Retrospect*, he traced his own uncertain journey, from farm boy to city mill worker, seizing opportunities for learning whenever possible, even teaching in a rural school, becoming involved with the Y.M.C.A., rising to its International Secretary, through it all becoming a devout Christian. He worked closely with Dwight L. Moody in raising funds for the great evangelist's two schools in Northfield, Massachusetts.

In his work with the Y.M.C.A., Lougee walked with the wealthy, with the Wanamakers, Sages, and Rockefellers of the day, knowing them on a personal basis. His successes in philanthropy brought an honorary Master of Arts Degree from Bates College in Lewiston, Maine, along with other recognitions. His name was in the New York City Social Register. His skill in fund raising took him as treasurer to the financially troubled Congregational Home Missionary Society, where debts were retired and budgets balanced during his six-year tenure.

He was at that post when the Eaton brothers came by. He remembered that it was a very busy day to fit into his schedule two men from Montana. But he found time, and as they shared their vision, something deep within responded. "I seemed," he recalled, "to see in (the Institute) the culmination of my life's work."[4] That led to his resignation from the Congregational Board and retirement to his farm in Candia, New Hampshire. There he would serve as the Institute's Eastern Representative, corresponding with thousands of potential donors.

Following a visit to Billings in the fall of 1914, Lougee prepared a full report "To the Many Friends of the Institute Throughout the Country."[5] He had nothing but praise for the little school, now in its 6th year. He was impressed with the Polytechnic's location at the center of "the great growing Northwest." The campus, "overlooking the beautiful and fertile valley of the Yellowstone," was obviously well planned for future growth.

The Dalton adding machine class stands outside Eaton Hall.

Auto mechanics class.

The Easterner was especially impressed with the youth he met. "I have never seen a more promising class of students in any school and one can readily see in them the future leaders of this great empire." Everything about the Poly was "life and business."

> The harvesting of crops on the farm was in full blast; some of the farm boys were just returning from the State Fair with upwards of fifty premiums won on farm products, boys were at work in the quarry and hauling rock for new buildings; the girls of the domestic science department were busily engaged in canning vegetables, fruits, jellies, and preserves.... All the work of the farm, general repair work about the building, waiting on tables in the dining room, the milking of cows, care of hogs and chickens, and the janitor work is done by students earning their way through school.

Along with the heavy emphasis on "practical education," the Polytechnic did not neglect the classroom, offering courses in Agriculture, Preparation in Engineering, the Normal and Commercial Departments, the Conservatory of Music, the Academy, and the College. The last offered instruction equivalent to the Freshman and Sophomore years in standard colleges. Participation was also important in Athletics and Physical Training, in the literary and musical groups, in training for citizenship through the Polytechnic State and religious nurture in the Polytechnic Church.

Lougee was especially pleased with the "spiritual tone" of the campus, finding it to be "the most noteworthy feature of the entire school." (p.3). He was also impressed with the Institute's close management, making every dollar count, having its own United States Post Office with the postmaster's salary of $1,000 going to the school. "One dollar," he concluded, "will go as far at the Polytechnic as ten dollars does at many similar institutions." (p.3).

The Institute's need for more donors was apparent, as well as the urgent requirement for additional buildings. He was glad to see ground broken while he was there for a Y.M.C.A. boy's dormitory—later Kenney Hall. The erection of a new dining hall and kitchen was another necessity, to replace "utterly inadequate" facilities. New barns and farm equipment were also a "must," to generate more income for the school. Such new construction, he figured, would run around $35,000, but would double the Institute's efficiency.

Harry D. Biddinger , Head and later owner, of Billings Business College.

Arthur Kline was a veteran teacher and Polytechnic administrator.

Alden Hall

Willis Lougee's first visit to Billings would confirm his suspicions that his final years might well be given to the school by the Yellowstone. Besides the cause, big enough for several lifetimes, there was the place, the valley from the Rimrocks, the patchwork of farms and multitude of haystacks, bathed in the fading glories of a western sunset. "There is something wonderfully inspiring in the atmosphere," he told a Chamber of Commerce luncheon. "It makes one feel that he would like to come here and stay always."[6]

His speech that day stirred the audience sufficiently to be reported on the front page of the *Billings Daily Tribune*, along with the war news.[7] The Poly's drive for $100,000 had fallen short of the goal and he urged the region to respond, with assurances that Eastern friends would provide equal amounts. East of the Mississippi, he declared, Billings was best known for its Polytechnic Institute, for a school with a bright future. He had corresponded with John Losekamp and shared the visionary merchant's dream that one day Billings would be the great educational center of the Northwest.

CAMPUS EXPANSION

Willis Lougee's visit seemed to stir new activity for the $100,000 campaign. I.D. O'Donnell, who had followed Losekamp as board president, was in Washington, D.C. when he wired a commitment of $2,500, adding a tract of land valued at $1,000. Another anonymous gift of $1,000 was reported, along with smaller donations. Mid-October brought a visitor from the Congregational Education Society in Boston. His main message, supported with illustrations from other states, was that the city and region must get behind their school if they expected significant support from back East.

Dr. F.M. Sheldon had arrived on the North Coast Limited for an overnight stay and meeting with the Polytechnic campaign team. He assured his audience that the Institute was well known in Massachusetts, that, in fact, "Billings Polytechnic is being watched by a surprising number of middle west and New England people....interested in knowing what Billings people are going to do to help their school....Be assured, the Polytechnic will pay back to the town more in actual money than the town ever will put into it."[8]

Though the desired goals seemed always beyond reach, regional support and Eastern benefactors kept the doors open and launched the Institute on a period of campus expansion. Kimball Hall was followed by the opening of Prescott Commons in 1916, providing much needed boarding facilities. Amos L. Prescott's initial gift of $50 ballooned into the major donation for the handsome sandstone building, with a large paneled common room, wooden beamed ceiling and large fireplaces at each end. For decades to come, it would be at the heart of campus life, for meals and social occasions, and the scene of the annual Candlelight Suppers.

Losekamp Conservatory, as noted earlier, was started in 1917 and occupied two years later. The modified Collegiate Gothic style added a dimension of dignity and grace to the campus. It still is a preferred building to be featured in college publications. Housing the Music Department, Losekamp Conservatory provided practice and classrooms and an auditorium, the scene through the years of required chapel, assemblies, drama productions, musicals, recitals, and other events. The Losekamp basement contained the Jesse Kirkpatrick Memorial Library.

The bare-bones gymnasium, first dedicated in 1912, acquired a sandstone facing and a more permanent appearance. It was renamed the Gymnasium and Armory, where students drilled with the country's entrance into World War I. The cornerstone for Kenney Hall was laid in May of 1918 and finally occupied in 1921. Asa W. Kenney of Lakewood, New Jersey was the major donor with a gift of $5,000. It was designed to house 50 boys, with a floor dedicated to Y.M.C.A. activities. Technology Hall was completed in 1922, a commodious sandstone structure containing offices, classrooms, laboratories, and the school's maintenance department.

Campus expansion at the Polytechnic caught the attention of the Deer Lodge paper. With the demise of the College of Montana, the *Silver State* for July 19, 1917 was happy to describe developments in Billings as a "great forward movement....in the heart of the Midland empire." New buildings in various states of planning and construction set a pace not seen in the state institutions and presaged one of the "best equipped educational institutions in the great Northwest." In the paper's view, there was ample room for "a great independent university" in Montana and the Polytechnic appeared to be on the way.

Along with the new buildings came additional land, with the acquisition of the Clanton Estate, increasing the campus to 287 acres. It was an impressive accomplishment, especially given the hard times following the collapse of the homestead frontier. Drought and the postwar depression brought declining prices for agricultural products, diminishing markets, and vanishing credit. Banks that had multiplied during the generous years now were closing by the score. Montana was the only state to lose population during the 1920s, as some 60,000 disappointed homesteaders, among others, looked for greener pastures elsewhere.

THE WAR YEARS

Meanwhile, the war that helped to close the College of Montana and leave Montana Wesleyan crippled but surviving also brought major adjustments to the Billings campus. Polytechnic had 134 boys in the service, leaving many chairs empty, eight of whom did not return. In proportion to population, Montana at large sent more soldiers to the Western Front and had more fatalities than any other state in the Union.

The campus also reflected the strong response on the home front to the war effort— the surge in patriotism, the conservation of needed resources, the purchase of Liberty Loan Bonds. The *Polygraph* for May 4, 1918 reported that the school had gone "gloriously" over the top in the third drive. Pledges of $3,800 were well in excess of the $2,500 goal. By that time, there was also a lively interest on campus in the proposed League of Nations, with the student publication firmly behind President Woodrow Wilson.

But wartime was most evident in an altered way of life at the Institute, one combining an emphasis upon military efficiency, patriotic values, with "growth in grace amid Christian surroundings." "Such is the life of every student at the Polytechnic-" *The Poly* for 1919 affirmed, "not at stated intervals, nor appointed times, but every day and every hour." (p. 20).

In an article titled "A Day at the Polytechnic," *The Poly* detailed the student's day beginning at 6:30 A.M., when "through the silent barrack halls the shrill, clear tones of *Reveille* call the sleepy boy from his dreams." Following roll call there are "setting-up exercises," similar to those at West Point, to assure a strong, healthy cadet, with a manly bearing. Rooms are then cleaned and inspected before breakfast, after which comes classes until 11:20, when all students march to chapel.

More drills after chapel prepare the young cadet for the welcome noon meal at 12:30, "a plain, simple, but healthful dinner," to which he gives "full justice." The afternoon is filled with guard duty, class-room work, and then an exchange of uniforms for athletic attire and the practice field. Following supper, there is some time for visiting before the "Call to Quarters" and study. An assembly in the Armory for inspection caps the day, with return to rooms and the sound of Taps across the campus beneath the Rimrocks.

Wesleyan students had donned the dress of the state militia, drilled daily and gone on marches, but it seems like a moment in time in the Poly story, those days caught up in a world at war, when for the while the school assumed a somewhat different character. Still, the work of instruction went on in the Junior College, the Academy, the School of Commerce, Normal Training, School of Engineering, Vocational Training, and the Losekamp Conservatory. Students tended the farms in season, gave recitals, learned to paint or speak in public, studied the Domestic Arts. In Athletics, the spring of 1918 brought baseball, a new coach, and hopes of beating the City High School.

Special events on campus during the war years included the lay-ing of the cornerstone of the Y.M.C.A. building, later named Kenney Hall, noted above. It was on May 4, 1918, a full day of activities, with speakers at morning chapel and then the dedication ceremonies at 3:30 P.M. I.D. O'Donnell, Board chair, presided, with dignitaries present from the state and international Y.M.C.A. to bring greetings and lend importance to the occasion. Later, the basement of Kenney would serve as a social center, with two lanes for bowling and Kampus Kave equipped with a large fireplace.

That fall, early October, brought to Billings and the Polytechnic a visitor whose brief stay would long be remembered. Popular ex-President Theodore Roosevelt was on a rousing western tour, stirring wartime passions, while promoting bond sales. There was also a critical congressional election in November. The frustrated Colonel, nearing

60, had been denied the opportunity of raising and commanding a volunteer force in Europe, as he had in Cuba. In lieu of that, the tour provided a "bully pulpit," lest no one mistake where he stood.

Early on October 5, he arrived on the Burlington, accompanied by Chamber president Frank B. Connelly and other dignitaries. Breakfast featured trout and then a full day of eight speeches, one of which was given on the Poly campus. It was the last delivered by the "incomparable Teddy" on a college occasion. "This is the kind of school," he affirmed, "that builds character and trains for the highest type of leadership. It is out from these vast open spaces of the northwest and from the valleys of these magnificent mountains yonder that the big, broad-minded, virile leaders of America must come."[9]

It is not recorded, but that must have brought both strong applause and tears of joy for the Eaton brothers. For that was precisely the vision they had for their struggling school. The former president's words would be inscribed on a large stone that stands near the entrance to the Bair Family Student Center.

Other speeches followed, some small talk with old friends, how he had found healing in the West following the deaths of his wife and mother, and the resolve to embark on a career that took him to the White House. It was for him and his audiences a truly "bully" day, one that ended at 7 P.M. when he boarded the Northern Pacific for the trip back home to Oyster Bay. Within a year, he would be dead, but those words, now at Rocky Mountain College, remain, a bit of vision from yesterday, something for today's students to read and ponder, as they go their way.

THE SECOND DECADE

The dedication of the Losekamp Conservatory was another important milestone, launching the Institute into the postwar years. The first use came on Easter Sunday, 1919, when a large audience filled the auditorium to hear special music and a sermon by the college pastor. Dedication occurred during Commencement Week, on May 27, with a full program of music and speakers. The main address was given by President James M. Hamilton from Montana State College in Bozeman. "Five Minute Speeches" included those by founding trustees James R. Goss and William B. George. Board president I.D. O'Donnell presided.

The Polytechnic Orchestra of 1916.

photo by K.F. Roahen

Tyler Hall

Along with the new facility, Polytechnic's Music Department was coming of age, with frequent requests for downtown programs, well attended concerts and recitals, with the faculty in demand to concertize during the summer in towns around Eastern Montana and in Wyoming. John Losekamp would have found ample compensation for all his efforts in the handsome new building and the quality of programs it housed. Over the years, traditions would build for excellence in music at the college beneath the Rims.

The Conservatory dedication in 1919 was only a part of a full week of activities at the Polytechnic Institute. Beyond the Baccalaureate Service and Commencement Exercises, there were Junior and Senior Class plays, Domestic and Fine Arts exhibits, a recital by the Department of Oratory, a benefit concert by the Eagle and Alpha Literary Societies, the Annual May Day Celebrations, and Class Day exercises by the 10 graduates.

There was also at some point in the week the Service of Silence on the Rims, observed at the opening and closing of school each year. Adapted from one the Lewis Eatons had seen at the Isle of Shoals in New England, it involved the "silent files of students slowly wend(ing) their way to the little out-of-doors temple upon the side of the rims, and there looking down upon a valley rich in beauty and fertility and guarded by the snow-capped mountains."[10] The setting and the silence made for a sense of awe, for something of the sacred, becoming a tradition that mattered over the years.

Such occasions were in keeping with an important dimension of life at the Polytechnic, namely, that of religious nurture. As noted earlier, a Polytechnic Church was one of the first organizations on campus, utilizing the services of the local Congregational minister, providing for chapels and vespers on a regular basis. It was the school's emphasis upon Christian values that appealed strongly to Willis Lougee, along with the open door, self-help approach to learning. He wrote in his *Diary* that "the ideals are lived up to a far greater extent than in any other school I have known anything about."[11]

He had spent four months at the Institute during 1915–16, replacing Ernest Eaton during his long convalescence from surgery. Following a more brief stay in early 1920, he returned to his farm in New Hampshire, only to have it burn and take the lives of his wife and sister-in-law. In his grief, he remembered, "I went and spent the summer (in Billings) with the students whom I had learned to love so well."[12] Somehow the Polytechnic was a place of healing, for when his second wife died unexpectedly, he returned to the campus once more to make it, in the main, his home. His "Lougee League" became a major presence for Christian witness and service.

Eastern Representative, Board member, honorary Institute president, Willis Lougee chose to live in student housing during his times on campus. In the view of *The Poly* for 1921, "It is really in the close friendly contact with young people that Mr. Lougee's influence is most felt. Every one who comes to know him intimately loves him as a true friend." There is no record of the many thousands in gifts he brought to the Polytechnic as part of the several million he raised in Christian and philanthropic work during his career. In Billings and elsewhere, the slightly built Vermonter stood tall in the esteem of those who knew him. Willis Eugene Lougee, "the Poly's Best Friend," died in 1935. One street and a small park in West Billings bear his name.

Along with religion, the Polytechnic Seal was inscribed with other markers of institutional purpose, namely, culture, industry, health, skill, and patriotism. It became customary for graduates each year to "pass down" the Seal to the next class, thus reaffirming directions for life on campus. The pursuit of culture was encouraged in course offerings, in the activities of the several literary societies, in the emphasis upon music, art, drama, in featuring student poetry and prose in *The Poly*, among other ways.

Good work habits also mattered, if the "Open Door" was to make a difference for those who entered it. Most students who came did not need convincing, especially those who were desperate for the opportunity the school offered, those who arrived nearly penniless, some without adequate clothing for the winter months. So they were found diligent in their duties on the farms, in the quarry preparing stones for a building, in the auto tractor department learning a trade, in other activities on a busy campus.

The Polytechnic's concern for health surfaced early in the building of a gymnasium, in the physical education requirements, and in a well-rounded athletic program for a fledgling, struggling school. News about the various team efforts regularly headlined *The Polygraph*, especially when the school prevailed over City High School or arch rival Montana Wesleyan, later Intermountain Union College.

Skill was deemed another essential, that the workman would be worthy of his hire. For the founders of the Polytechnic, that began with a knowledge of the basics, with reading, writing, speaking, use of numbers. That meant for many students a year or two in the Academy before advancing to the Junior College and more specialized learning. Meanwhile, patriotism, the last of the goals inscribed on the Seal, involved not only love of country, but preparation to serve as active and enlightened citizens. So early on the Poly State provided experience with self-government. In daily chapels and assemblies, the Eatons and others stressed these fundamentals of a sound education, the building blocks of a useful life.

GROWTH MIDST TRIALS

The new residential facilities made possible some growth in the school, with enrollments reaching 200 late in the decade. The paving of the Poly road earlier (1920) had also improved access from the town, especially during harsh winter weather that had tended to isolate the campus. *The Billings Polygraph* for October 8, 1928 reported over 200 registered, with the strong likelihood that there would be more students coming as soon as harvesting operations permitted. They were from all over the Midland Empire and beyond, from Montana, Wyoming, the Dakotas, Washington and Texas. There was even one student from Massachusetts.

The purchase of the Billings Business College in October, 1927 added nearly 100 students to the total enrollment. The school had been started in 1910, incorporated in 1916, bought and operated by W.H. Bergherm in 1920. He remained as principal of the accredited institution, with the Polytechnic adding college level courses to the commercial curriculum. Campus faculty traveled in town for afternoon and evening classes in areas like English Composition, Literature, Spanish, Psychology, and Public Speaking. A free bus service was provided for Billings students wishing to study on the campus.

Lewis Eaton was pleased with these developments, commenting in the *Polygraph* (October 8, 1928) that the "general growth of the

Polytechnic and the enlargement of its work has made necessary a number of additions to the faculty." They included two in the English Department, one of whom was Lincoln J. Aikens, moving from an academy in Maine to serve the Poly with distinction before relocating to Dawson County Junior College and then Eastern Montana Normal School. He was one of several in the next few years, teachers like Charlie Martin and Herb Klindt, who joined veterans like Arthur O. Kline and Emma Johnson in providing the school needed continuity in its instructional program.

Old grads from those days will remember other teachers who left enduring memories, earning minimal salaries, living in the dormitories, taking their meals at Prescott Commons, supplied with milk from the dairy and other produce from the farms. Of 24 faculty and staff listed in the *Billings Polygraph* of October 12, 1934, only six did not have a dormitory address. Typical of small schools, teachers ranged widely over their assigned fields of study. For Herb Klindt, fresh from coaching at Clearwater High School in Florida, the assignment was Athletic Director, four sports, and resident proctor in a dormitory. He was spared, however, having to teach a Methodist Sunday School class, which had been part of his duties in Clearwater.

But if the *modus vivendi* of Poly teachers reflected a notable commitment to the institution, there were promising signs of better times ahead as the decade drew to a close. The Forward Movement Fund for $150,000 launched early in 1927 was a resounding success, exceeding the goal. Contributions came from nearly every state in the Union, with Connecticut and Massachusetts leading in subscriptions, but with the largest donation of $12,000 coming from California.

That triggered an announcement of plans for two new dormitories, accommodating 100 students, at $50,000 each. According to *The Billings Polytechnic* of October 21, 1927, the school was now attracting youth from more than ten states. It was becoming widely known as the college that adapted instruction to fit individual needs. This fund drive would generate sufficient support for the construction of Tyler Hall.

More auspiciously, it seemed, the Polytechnic Board next embarked on an ambitious Endowment and Enlargement Campaign, to raise $1,500,000 over the next five years. The initial focus would be upon the Chicago and New England areas, upon familiar territory and old friends, though the effort would become nationwide in scope. Willis Lougee had been back home in New Bedford, Massachusetts, but returned to Billings to accompany Lewis Eaton in the new endeavor. They left for the East in January, 1928, for a three month cultivation in behalf of what was billed as the "Greater Polytechnic."[13]

The time seemed right, with what Lougee described as "the best corps of teachers" and "the finest group of students we have ever had." There was talk about moving toward a full college curriculum. So it was an enthusiastic group of students and teachers who gathered at the station to see Eaton and Lougee entrain for the East.

Their plan was to spend about three weeks in Chicago, including a visit with Dr. John A. Kirkpatrick, hopefully to raise $35,000 for the first unit of the Jesse Kirkpatrick Memorial Library. Then they would proceed to New York, before going to Boston and establishing campaign headquarters at Congregational House. Eaton would remain about three months, while Lougee would stay on indefinitely.

An early gift of $50,000 paid for Tyler Hall, the first building on campus to be funded in advance of construction. Ernest Eaton noted at the ground breaking ceremonies on October 26, 1928 that it was a good sign that the Endowment and Enlargement Campaign would succeed. The donor from Brookline, Massachusetts, later identified as Mrs. G.W. Mchaffey, made the contribution to honor her father, W. Graham Tyler, who had provided many scholarships for students to attend college.

The three story sandstone building, Gothic design, would accommodate 60 students, with an apartment for the House Mother. Fourteen self-help students worked on the project, assisting the masons and carpenters, among other duties. Stones from the quarry were cut by Matt Marshall, who had worked on all the Polytechnic buildings. Born in Austria, he had been employed by the Anaconda Copper Company in Butte before coming to Billings in 1908. From one enormous stone, the story goes, he chiseled all the blocks for Prescott Commons. Tyler was dedicated and occupied in 1930.

Girl's basketball team of 1920

Boy's football team of 1916.

TRANSITIONS ▧

Late fall of 1929 had brought disquieting news to the campus, as to the nation at large, about Black Thursday and the collapse of the stock market, the apparent end of an era of good times. But there were plans afoot at the Polytechnic for a big celebration of its 21st anniversary. With the Eatons away on fund raising trails, the Kiwanis Club, other organizations, and churches joined in planning and supporting an evening to be remembered. Invitations were mailed to over 400 friends of the school in the Midland Empire.

It happened on Tuesday, December 10th, an Anniversary Banquet packing Prescott Commons to overflowing, so that many faculty and students had to eat in the basement of Losekamp Conservatory. Everything on the menu came from the farms: turkeys, a variety of vegetables, dairy products, bread, honey, and fruits from the orchards. Ernest Eaton observed that there wasn't another college or university in the land that could duplicate that accomplishment.

Back in town, the brothers savored every moment of that evening, some introductions of the Poly family, talk of the past, hopes for the future, other speeches, songs by the Polytechnic chorus, and then what the audience had been waiting to hear—an update on the Endowment and Enlargement Campaign. There had been a major gift of $200,000 from an old friend, with total pledges of $340,000. The directors were confident that the goal of $1,500,000 was within reach.[14]

But as the Great Depression deepened, there was an added note of urgency in appeals from the school. It became necessary to put the campaign on hold and concentrate on gifts to meet current expenses. Friends, old and new, were challenged to consider a donation of $10 to meet the financial needs of the Institute for one hour, $100 for a student's tuition, $1,000 to endow a scholarship, and $2,000 to fund a loan program. Such help would enable the Polytechnic to accept more deserving students of the great Northwest. More than 2,000 had been turned away in 1929!

For those still with the means, $20,000 would acquire more fertile acreage, $25,000 with student labor to build another modern dormitory, $50,000 for a much needed gymnasium, engineering building, or chapel. Any of these could be constructed with stone from the quarry and student self-help at one half the actual cost.[15]

The anxious brothers continued their travels, with Ernest including California in his destinations. It was the place, over the years, where he sought rest and renewal for body and spirit.

Ernest also found some needed change in outlook with his career in state politics, serving several terms in the lower house of the state legislature before moving to the senate in 1930. He became president of that body in 1935 and later was elected to the office of Lieutenant Governor. He promoted educational concerns and was instrumental in framing the bill that established Eastern Montana Normal School.

While the hard times seemed to mock the brothers' vision of a large university beneath the Rims, serving the neglected youth of the Northwest, the life on campus had its compensations. The Polytechnic was not lacking for students as the waiting list lengthened, the farms were winning recognition, the Conservatory had a regular hour on KGHL, providing the community with fine music. Klindt-coached "Crusaders" in the various sports were working on an impressive record of victories. Other evidences of a lively campus were recorded in the *Polygraph*.

Then there were the traditions, the community memory of times and customs that mattered in the ongoing life of the school, notably the Candlelight Banquet, May Day, and the Silent Service during Commencement Week. "Moving Day" had an earlier version featuring a "symbolic supper" of sandwiches and coffee served on rough board tables. Ernest Eaton recalled the first setting, then music by the Polytechnic singers. A basketball game usually followed, before the move to a more "sumptuous banquet" at Prescott Commons, with speakers and appropriate toasts in honor of the occasion. The *Billings Polytechnic* (February 16, 1930) noted that the earlier observance had given way to "softer methods" and a more "civilized observance."

Such was the 23rd Candlelight Banquet on Saturday evening, January 30, 1932. In the midst of unprecedented economic crisis in the land, school and friends paused to savor what they had in common, food, ample and flavorful from Poly farms, times to recall, music by the Polytechnic orchestra, chorus, ensembles, the usual speeches including one by Preston B. Moss on "Polytechnic Pioneers." Ernest Eaton was there to remember "Departed Members" and to preside over the candle lighting ceremony. Doubtless, the warmth of fellow-ship followed participants out into the evening cold.

Summers found 75 student or so engaged in various self-help tasks, attending summer school, or enrolled at the camp at Beehive Ranch. That acreage outside of Absarokee had been purchased by Thomas O. Eaton with the family's move to Billings. It was an ideal location, with the Stillwater running through. "Beehive Camp," a promotional brochure assured, "has the fullest measure of Western ranch atmosphere. Here the boys are given everything to complete the fundamentals of life, natural, physical, mental, and spiritual training, all of which are needed to round out any youth's experience and education."[16]

CELEBRATION AND SORROW

It was in the worst of times for finding big gifts that the Polytechnic paused to observe its Silver Jubilee. May, 1933 was the appointed month, with various events and celebrations scheduled through Commencement Day, June 2nd. *The Billings Polygraph* for May 5 sounded an opening note:

> Twenty-five years ago the Polytechnic began its official life. Hundreds of students have crossed over its thresholds to catch new visions of service. During these years—years of joy and pleasure as well as of toil and trouble—the founders and early friends of the school have seen the campus develop out of a beet field into a spacious landscape of trees, shrubs, flowers, and lawns, amid which the eight permanent buildings stand as sentinels of a mighty advance. Alert, eager students clamor for admittance to this unique institution—advance post in the progress of American education.

Founder's Day was an important part of the 25th anniversary proceedings. It began with a convocation of all Polytechnic students, including those enrolled in the Business College, with devotional exercises and remarks on the significance of the occasion. There was a track meet in the afternoon, followed by a Tug-of-War between the two male literary societies. The Pioneers prevailed at the meet, but the Eagles got sweet revenge in pulling their straining adversaries into the upper irrigation ditch![17]

Less stressful was the picnic supper beside the Lily Pool. Wind and threatening rain moved the happy company inside to the Conservatory Recital Hall. There the Eatons, Board president I.D. O'Donnell, and other original trustees recalled the early days. They were Judge James R. Goss, Preston B. Moss, and William B. George. Moss would have the longest tenure, serving as treasurer from 1908 until his death in 1946. He almost had the satisfaction of seeing the paths of the predecessor institutions converge with Rocky Mountain College.

The ongoing struggle for resources led the Eatons to rethink some directions for their school. Actually, they explained, it was a "faint dream" they had from the beginning. In an interview early in 1934, Lewis outlined ways in which the Polytechnic could become a self-supporting institution. The main aim would be to expand the industrial departments, generating market income while providing employment for hundreds of students. He explained:

> One thing is certain—the Polytechnic must become a self-supporting institution. In time past we have begged for hundreds of thousands of dollars for the building of the school and the support of the student body. Times have changed. Opportunity must be given for worthwhile students to support themselves by remunerative industries. Generous friends have given us an abundance of productive land and they have supplied us with splendid buildings. We must not ask them to give us our food and clothing. The opportunity is ours to build a most unique institution.[18]

Noting that some initial investment would be required, Eaton viewed the Institute's future in terms of a marketing center—a breakfast food plant, a cottage cheese industry, a store for the sale of Polytechnic produce, a cannery to handle all kinds of fruits and vegetables. The green-gold label would become well known in the land. There would even be a woolen mill as a value-added industry to keep part of the wealth in the state. "The vision grows, " Eaton affirmed. "There is no limit to what can be done in manufacturing Montana products....It will make the Polytechnic itself the greatest school in the country. It is certainly an inspiration and it can be done!"[19]

The elder Eaton was not privileged to see that part of his dream pursued. A history of heart problems led to a fatal attack on March 14, 1934. He had been in his office the day before, performing various tasks, counseling with students, offering that friendship which over the years had encouraged them to go on. Never one to spare himself, his thoughts and energies were for the school until the end. Death came in the morning, in the quietness of his home.

Services were held at the Polytechnic chapel, his casket on the stage where he had so often presided. Students stood silently as honor guards and overflowed outside of the hall. Honorary pallbearers included trustees, heads of service clubs and educational institutions, as well as city officials. Burial was in Mountview Cemetery, not far from where his old friend and colleague, John Losekamp, lay. In another year, Willis Lougee would join him, these makers of the school beneath the Rims.

It was a staggering loss for the struggling school, a great emptiness for his family and brother, the Poly community, and a time of sadness for students from across the years. His death at 64 left a place which could not be filled by a mere closing of the ranks. So it often is with the lives that make a difference, whose fruits are more in the seeds that are planted than in the enjoyment of an eventual harvest.

Dining in Prescott Commons

Chapter Nine The Way to Union

" It looks as tho we are going to get some place with Poly yet.
God help us that we may save it and build on it for the future
generations of Midland Empire youth."
— *Rev. Cloyd Conner*

*Robert Frost's appearance on campus during Commencement Week
of 1934 was a welcome time in a season of sorrow.* The famous poet
had a married daughter in town, Robin Fraser, and combined a visit
with a Convocation speech, mostly reading some of his best-loved
poems. There were 13 graduates from the Junior College, nine from
the Academy, and 16 from the Business School. Ernest Eaton, now
president, presided at exercises.

While the brothers were serious about a self-supporting institution,
with expanded industrial departments and programs, they had also been
thinking about moving beyond the Junior College with a full liberal
arts curriculum. That was another "faint dream" not lost with the
years. By way of implementation, Dr. Wendell S. Brooks was called
to Billings that fall of 1934 as founding president of a "Liberal Arts
College." He had just resigned as head of Intermountain Union and
welcomed the new opportunity.

There was no time lost, as Brooks joined Ernest Eaton in Chicago
for a fund raising sweep of Eastern cities, including New York, Boston,
and Philadelphia among others. The plan now was to revive the
endowment effort, with a goal of one million dollars. Reports of large
donations to the Harvards and Yales spurred hopes that the worst of

the Depression was over. Initial activities produced $120,000 in cash and pledges, before two serious surgeries took Eaton again to California for what proved to be a nine month stay. Son Robert remembered that the family returned in time for the 1936 Commencement.

The campaign had been put on hold, to be renewed in 1938. Contacts in the East did result in a gift by the Alden Trust of Worcester, Massachusetts which led to the construction of Alden residence hall in 1937. That was the last of the permanent buildings, until the Paul M. Adams Memorial Library was occupied in 1959. A wooden structure, Montana Hall, was built in 1947 for classrooms and laboratory space and later demolished. Alden Hall ended an impressive record of accomplishment, given the hard times in Montana during the years between the wars.

The transition was complete from a beet field to an attractive college scene, sloping down from the commanding Rims. Where once a solitary tree stood sentinel over a barren place, hundreds of trees, shrubbery, lawns, and well-kept gardens provided an appealing setting for handsome buildings. Two of the old wooden dormitories remained for faculty housing, reminders of the school's infancy. The Polytechnic campus of the 1930s, hardly the biggest and best in the Northwest, was a testimony to vision, struggle, and courage, a place of purpose where once only sugar beets grew.

Back home from the fund raising trip, Dr. Brooks turned his attention to securing full accreditation for the Junior College. In 1925 the North Central Association of Colleges and Secondary Schools had accredited high school work. Subsequently, there were provisional steps, leading to an institutional self-study, review, and visit to the campus. Dean Frederick E. Bolton of the University of Washington received red carpet treatment, and was even invited to speak at chapel. Brooks traveled to Spokane in April, 1935 to meet with the Northwestern Association of Colleges and Universities. The result was most gratifying, with the Junior College receiving full accreditation "without qualification or limitation."[1]

That fall the dormitories were full and again in January for the spring semester. There were about 200 students on campus. The Candlelight Banquet drew a record 350 alumni, Poly Family, and friends, about overflowing Prescott Commons. The Jesse Kirkpatrick

Memorial Library, under the capable supervision of Emma Johnson, occupied the entire ground floor of Losekamp Conservatory. New lighting had been installed and additional stacks ordered to handle books from Intermountain Union, with total holdings now reaching 30,000. The Polytechnic Church, spanning the years, continued to prosper. Daily chapel remained a requirement.

Lewis Eaton would have been pleased with new marketing initiatives, notably the "Green and Gold" whole wheat breakfast food. That enterprise had originated in the basement of Prescott Commons, largely from the efforts of a student off a homestead near Roy, Montana. David Dunn returned after graduation to build the business. By the fall of 1935 a larger mill was needed and a new delivery truck to serve the Billings area. As the brothers intended, it was mainly a student operation— upkeep of the machinery, work in the milling, training in packaging and shipping, bookkeeping, general responsibility for a successful business.

One disappointment for the Eatons was the abandonment of the Poly State or Republic. For they believed deeply in the need of training for citizenship. Patriotism, as we have seen, was one of the cardinal objectives on the Institute's seal. The Republic had lapsed during the war years, when the Polytechnic became virtually a military school, with its own priorities, organizations, and disciplines. Attempts to revive the old order, with its three branches of government, elections and the like had been unsuccessful. At length, however, in the fall of 1936 efforts were fruitful in forming the Associated Students of the Billings Polytechnic Institute.

By the mid-1930s, the ranks of the old-timers had thinned to a handful. For the trustees, I.D. O'Donnell and P.B. Moss remained to guard memories of beginnings back in 1908. On the faculty, Emma Johnson matched the Eatons' tenure, having been with them since the Deer Lodge days. Arthur Kline had come to the Polytechnic from Indiana in 1910 to serve in various capacities, as head of the Commercial Department, in the business office, as postmaster and as registrar. "Daddy" Kline's death in the summer of 1935 was another deeply felt loss for the Institute.

Another familiar figure on campus, mentioned earlier, was a now aging Matt Marshall, master mason, lord of the college quarry, whose handiwork was evident in the several buildings. He lived alone in one of the old dormitories, but counted numerous friends among young and old alike. Cane in hand, candy in his pockets for campus children, he would ride the college bus into town and invariably declare upon his return: "It's good to be home." The kindly stone mason died at age 79, in January, 1939.

POLYTECHNIC INTERMOUNTAIN

The period from 1936 to 1947 would see both the best and worst of times for the Polytechnic Institute. Enrollments would soar on the campus and in the Business College, approaching 1,000 registrations by 1940. With the country's entrance into the war, however, the bottom fell out, leaving a scattering of students with a skeleton operation, and a school trying hard to hang on until peace returned. President Eaton's task during these years was complicated by recurring illness and the responsibilities of public office added to the daily routine.

But it was nature's intervention in the fortunes of a sister institution that would shape developments during the final years of the Polytechnic. Intermountain Union College, as we have seen, lost its Helena campus to earthquakes in 1935 and was unable to secure a foothold in Great Falls during its relocation there. Its fate mattered to the Polytechnic president, as part of a larger concern for Protestant higher education in Montana. Painful memories also lingered for Ernest Eaton of what had happened in Deer Lodge, and his desire to save Intermountain prompted an invitation to come to Billings.*

Intermountain trustees had discarded any thought of rebuilding in Helena and were weighing the possibilities of affiliation with

---

* It appears that the Polytechnic had considered at least one other merger possibility, with a church-related college in South Dakota. An undated document in the RMC archives is titled "A Tentative Proposal for the Merger of the Billings Polytechnic Institute And Redfield College." Since it refers to the fairly recent founding of Eastern Montana Normal School (1927), it suggests a date of around 1930. Redfield College and Seminary, affiliated with the General Conference of German Speaking Congregations, would relocate to Billings, be renamed Billings College and handle the college department. Each institution would retain its governing board. Further information on the proposal was not available.

another institution. Billings seemed to offer the best solution. Intermountain's Dr. Cecil L. Clifford explained the trustees' decision:

> The Polytechnic campus was chosen as the site for the continuation of Intermountain because it was thought that here the purpose for which the school was founded, to maintain a Christian school offering a general education, could be best carried on. We are not here for a trial period, but to work out a program to the mutual advantage of the schools and this we expect to accomplish.[2]

Actually the affiliation was not viewed as final; rather, the two governing boards would monitor developments and, if indicated, consummate relationships, which happened in 1939. Meanwhile, Intermountain's role was to conduct the four year Liberal Arts curriculum, securing a resident dean to supervise the program. Dr. Clifford retained oversight as Acting Dean and proceeded to fill the campus position. Reverend Joseph S. Pennepacker came from a Methodist pastorate in Rhode island, arriving with his son by bus, before the opening of the school in September, 1936.

The new dean was no stranger to Montana, having served a Methodist church in Libby for several years. His first housing was in Tyler Hall, while the rest of the family, upon their arrival, found rooms in another dormitory. It made for a good introduction to campus life but lacked in domestic considerations.* Dean Pennepacker soon discovered that in addition to his administrative duties there was need to teach a class or two. Like other clergy on the faculty, he would also be supplementing a slim salary with weekend preaching.

Most of the Intermountain faculty, staff, and students had scattered elsewhere, but a few made the move to Billings, including George Gloege in Chemistry and several students. They were welcomed to the various campus organizations and encouraged to share their own customs and traditions. One of Wesleyan vintage to be adopted was the annual football banquet. Doubtless it became a time for stories about Intermountain Panther and Polytechnic Crusader rivalries, of hard-fought games, gridiron heroes, and conference championships won.

---

* Coming from New Jersey in January, 1959, the writer and family spent the first two weeks on campus in the basement of Alden Hall.

1936 Track champions.

The 1934 Debate team

These would be the better years, cut short by the coming of another world war. The signs for Polytechnic-Intermountain seemed good—solid gains in enrollment, another new dormitory, the affiliation agreement consummated, the three denominations (Methodist, Presbyterian, Congregational) taking a new interest in the school. The trustees resumed a major campaign to raise $1,250,000 for endowment and campus enlargement purposes. There was, then, some reason for hope, though lean times remained for faculty, staff, and families.

Most encouraging were the gains in enrollment, virtually doubling the student body between 1937 and 1939. *The Polygraph* for September 22, 1937 noted registrations of 347 with more expected to arrive. By 1939 Registrar Lincoln J. Aikens was reporting to the Montana Congregational Conference that over 700 students were in attendance.[3] They were in the four collegiate schools, Polytechnic-Intermountain, School of Technology, Losekamp Conservatory of Music, Business College, and from the Academy. President Eaton fully expected 1,000 students by the new decade. Graduates also reflected the change, from 81 in 1937 to 128 in 1939.

There was growth in most of the departments, but the Business College remained the heaviest enrolled. Purchased by the Polytechnic in 1927, it had prospered under the leadership of H.D. Biddinger (1928), registering over 400 students annually by 1938. Located in the Empire Building, it was "modern in every respect," with "machine equipment that is unsurpassed in this part of the country."[4] The popular school attracted students from a range of states, from Iowa and Kansas to Idaho and Washington. It had the reputation for placing graduates in good paying jobs, especially with the federal government in Washington.

The dedication services for Alden Hall, housing another 52 male students, also seemed to signal better times. It was a sunny Monday, September 12, 1938 when the campus community, along with town leaders gathered first at Losekamp Conservatory for worship, music, and an address by Dean Pennepacker. They then assembled at the new dormitory for further remarks by Board president Harry Carpenter and Mr. Paul Morgan from Worcester, Massachusetts representing the George I. Alden Trust. I.D. O'Donnell was also there to reflect upon three decades in the life of this school he had helped to establish.

Morgan was accompanied by his wife, daughter and son-in-law. The Alden Trust had been founded by the late George I. Alden, a college professor in Worcester. In addition to gifting the new dormitory, the Trust had provided support for starting the School of Technology and other improvements totalling nearly $100,000. It was, thus, a major benefactor and the object of further requests by President Eaton. Morgan and family stayed on for several days, attended a reception in their honor, and enjoyed a pleasant Montana autumn.

Earlier that year of 1938, P.B. Moss recalled at the Candlelight Banquet: "I remember that Billings residents scoffed 30 years ago when I said that a college would be founded in the city."[5] To be sure, it had been and continued to be a relentless struggle, but Guy L. Barnes, Secretary of the Board, could report total assets of $1,446,996. The school could claim 350 acres of irrigated farmland, orchids, gardens, field plots, and dairy, supplying the dining hall and faculty homes. In addition, there were 1,000 acres at Beehive on the upper Stillwater.

Some Billings residents would still scoff at talk of a university with several thousand students, but Moss and other believers would not discount what the next 30 years might produce. Meanwhile, there was need for additional land, new dormitories for the region's needy youth, a library and classroom building, faculty housing, a greenhouse and seed house, a printing and bindery building, a hospital and numerous other improvements. There was no dearth of plans for things to come.

Moved by such an agenda, the Polytechnic Board voted at its February, 1938 meeting to renew the effort to raise $1,250,000 for endowment and campus enlargements. With an end date of 1941, the president was "authorized to pursue the campaign with all diligence."[6] Health apparently remained a concern, for Ernest Eaton stopped off at the Mayo Clinic in Rochester, Minnesota on his way back East to promote the campaign. The larger problem, however, remained the Great Depression. Despite all the New Deal initiatives, there were still millions unemployed and money remained tight. Only the coming of World War II would end the nation's long economic woes. But that would also spell near disaster for the Billings school.

The tentative affiliation of the Polytechnic and Intermountain stirred new interest in the three related denominations. In August of 1937, the Methodist Education Board and Annual Conference endorsed support for the new venture. The following year, in November, representatives of the three national boards met on campus and were impressed with the progress made. Accordingly, they approved making the affiliation a permanent one.

That triggered action by the two governing boards, to consummate the relationships between the two schools. *The Billings Polygraph* for February, 1939 reported that the new agreement created the Liberal Arts College as a separate entity, to be known as the Polytechnic-Intermountain College. It was to have its own officers and board of control, with four representatives from each of the trustee boards. The long view envisioned a complete merger of the two schools.

The Billings Polytechnic Institute's name and management was not effected, since it owned and controlled the property involved. It continued its supervision of the School of Technology, the Business College, Losekamp Conservatory of Music, and the Academy. The athletic teams, glee clubs, debate squads and other groups would continue to compete under the name of the Billings Polytechnic Institute.

Life on campus continued with its stringencies and compensations. Faculty came and went, each fall producing replacements for those not willing or able to cope with conditions. Fortunately, the overworked dean could depend upon an ample pool of unemployed teachers in the nation. For those who stayed, the stalwarts of the Poly vision, there were good times along with the seasons to try the spirit. The students mattered and there was also the place— the invitation to field and stream or the mountains, rugged and overwhelming, offering perspective, solitude, something of inner peace.

Five houses were added on "Faculty Circle" off 17th Street, moved from a mining camp at Nye, Montana. They provided some escape from crowded dormitory quarters for those not able to afford residences in town. Alumni from those years remember teachers who really cared, favorite "profs," who made a real difference in their lives. It was, indeed, the School of the Open Door, for not a few who entered had only the means to get there, with only change in their pockets. More than one lacked proper clothing for the winter months, fortunate that there was a teacher, one with little money to spare, buying a coat for them.

Even the dedicated could not have stayed had not the Polytechnic provided food—meals at the Prescott Commons, groceries from the store in its basement, bread, cereals, preserves and the like, trips to the farm for milk, eggs, and chicken, wherever supplies were to be found. Faculty teenagers, otherwise known as "faculty brats," grabbed opportunities to babysit or wait on tables, especially at Candlelight Banquets, garnering a few coins for candy money.

Tough times did not dampen a lively spirit on campus, whether in the various organizations or in the enjoyments students found in being together. Sports were popular and figured prominently in the pages of *The Polygraph*. The school fielded teams in baseball, track, football, and basketball. It was the last that had the largest following, with the Crusaders completing three consecutive seasons as Conference champions. There was also a girls team at the Business College, evidently less successful in the winning column. *The Poly* for 1937 observed that the players displayed good sportsmanship throughout the season. "The team always returned with a smile and a determination to do better in the next game." (p. 66)

Events at Losekamp Conservatory included performances by band, orchestra, chorus, quartets, trios, and the production in 1937 of Gilbert and Sullivan's popular operetta "H.M.S. Pinafore." That year saw the merger of the two drama societies, the Polythespians and the Black Masque into the Masqued Thespians. The four Literary Societies added their considerable contributions in sponsoring contests and dances, promoting both literature and school spirit, encouraging leadership and self-expression. Affairs of government were left with the Associated Students of Billings Polytechnic Institute.

In addition to the organized activities, there were individual pastimes like bowling on the two lanes in Kenney Hall basement, socializing in the adjacent Kampus Kave, walks into town, outings in the mountains or at Beehive. From the beginning, when other diversions failed, there were the antics common to college life, ingenious ways of challenging rules and regulations. Sometimes it could involve a budding romance, a hapless student caught on a fire-escape in a vain attempt to see his girl friend. The Polytechnic was no exception to that historic role of the coed campus in the production of wedding bells.

Few students in those best of years would forget the religious dimension of life on campus. Daily chapel might seem a bit much, but they could bring memorable speakers, as on that October 28, 1937 when the great Quaker leader, E. Stanley Jones, moved the audience with his message. Some traditions were fading, but the Service of Silence still found faculty and students gathering on the Rims. The Polytechnic Congregational Church was one of 24 in the city. Whether at worship, study, or play, there was something about the school that seemed to redeem the hard times, a sense of family, a feeling of home within the open door.

END OF AN ERA

The war that began in September, 1939 brought sweeping changes for life in the country. It signaled the end of the Great Depression as America once more became the granary and supplier of Allied war needs. In Montana there was also a return to ample moisture, triggering good times on the farms and ranches. That meant more students from the rural areas and elsewhere, and enrollments at Polytechnic-Intermountain for the year 1940–41 topped 1,000 for the first time in the school's history! That happy occasion merited banner headlines in *The Billing Polygraph* for May 23, 1941.

Mainstays of campus life continued to shape the Polytechnic-Intermountain experience—winning teams, the literary societies, Lougee League, daily chapel, socializing in Kampus Kave, self-help work on the farm and elsewhere. The Candlelight Supper remained the big event of the year for the school family, drawing capacity crowds to Prescott Commons, feeding memories of the past 30 years and more. That would soon change, but for the while, as the Polytechnic crossed over into a new decade, there was a sense of miles traveled since the early days.

The main worry remained the lack of adequate resources. The major fund drive for endowment and enlargement purposes, resurrected in 1938, produced a new promotional piece, *Youth From Plains and Mountains Build a College*. It restated the case for the Polytechnic, stressing the students' role in the construction of buildings, along with testimonials by prominent Americans. Scheduled to end in 1941, the campaign attracted some Eastern support, including an annual contribution of $5,000 by the Alden Trust, but nothing in the range of gifts needed to achieve the goal.

Meanwhile, Ernest Eaton opted to pursue his career in politics, building upon his years in the lower and upper branches of the legislature, running successfully in 1940 for Lieutenant Governor. Doubtless, time in Helena provided a needed change of pace, but it added major responsibilities, especially when Governor Sam Ford was out of state and Eaton was called to the capitol. It figured in his correspondence with Eastern contacts, that he could not get away as much as he would like, due to state business and the urgencies at the school.

Early in the new decade, while the war spread in Europe and the debate here mounted between the isolationists and the internationalists, the Polytechnic-Intermountain gained full accreditation by the Northwest Association of Schools and Colleges. That ended a year to year status for the Liberal Arts Program. President Eaton, Dean Pennepacker, and Professor Lincoln Aikens attended the March, 1940 meeting in Spokane, Washington. Commencement in May found some decline in graduates, down to 108 in the Polytechnic's five schools.

The summer of 1940, however, saw an increase in Summer School enrollment and a new program in flight training offered by the Civil Aeronautics Authority. About 30 students had registered with more expected. The course was designed to provide instruction for a private pilot's license. There was no military obligation, but students completing the program were eligible for additional training "under whatever auspices this training may be offered."[7] It became customary when a student pilot completed his first solo flight to be thrown unceremoniously into the Lily Pond between Science Hall and Losekamp Conservatory.

Faculty turnover that fall involved Lincoln Aikens, who had also served as registrar. He had survived the Depression years, but with salaries still in arrears, he took a position as dean at the newly opened Dawson County Junior College in Glendive. Later he would move to Eastern Montana College, serving as a senior administrator. Meanwhile, *The Billings Polygraph* reported an enrollment increase in all five schools, with the Business College registering 175 students.

A new venture in Polytechnic industries, one hardly foreseen by Lewis Eaton, involved the production of oil and gas. With the supervision of a veteran oil man, a small building was constructed with equipment to refine oil and gas. Crude oil from Elk Basin was hauled on Polytechnic trucks. *The Billings Polygraph* for December 6, 1940 reported production of approximately 15 barrels of gasoline and 7 of truck fuel, along with kindred by-products. When fully operational, it was expected that the little refinery would net $100 a day. As with the farm, products would be used on campus and sold in the region. "In some cases," according to the *Polygraph* "it may be used in the barter system with farmers who will supply wheat for the Polytechnic mill." (p. 2).

The Green-Gold Milling Co. was housed in a large, attractive stucco building across the road from the campus. It represented reality in the Eaton's self-help ambitions - built and operated by students! Initial profits had been invested in enlarging the mill and purchasing new machinery to merchandize a more varied product. A delivery truck carried Green and Gold cereals and pancake flour far afield, to Sydney and Glendive, Red Lodge and Roundup and points in-between. By 1941 the mill was turning a tidy profit, old bills paid, looking forward to brisk sales during the winter months.

The last year before Pearl Harbor and America's entrance into the war saw normal activity on the campus, the Crusaders battling for another Conference championship, a spirited contest for "campus sweetheart," the 45 member Chapel Choir on tour, the literary societies promoting dances and plays, the school's debate squad afield on several trips, addressing the current topic: "Resolved that freedom of speech and press should be denied to representatives and agents in the United States of those nations where like liberty is denied."[8] It proved to be a banner year for the Poly debaters, placing first in the state competition.

Commencement 1941 saw a further decline in graduates, with 75 receiving degrees and diplomas from the several schools. Boyd F. Baldwin, Intermountain Union alumnus of 1927, took the occasion for some reminiscing and a call for the transfer of old loyalties to the new creation, with a note of optimism for the future. "As a college," he observed, "we build upon the past, we do not live in the past....With our help, coupled with the native resources of the campus, we can develop upon the rimrock campus one of the finest centers for collegiate training in the northwest."[9]

Baldwin welcomed the graduates to the ranks of the loyal alumni, encouraging them to become supporters of their Alma Mater. But many that day would soon be caught up in the winds of war, some not to return from distant battlefields. At the Poly halls and classrooms were emptied, activities curtailed, self-help programs with no students to work them, an institution not unfamiliar with struggle, now facing its most perilous hour.

EDGE OF SURVIVAL

There had been some thinning of the ranks through faculty and student enlistments in the Armed Services. In fact, during the previous two years, nearly 100 "Polyites" had entered the army, navy, air corps, or marines. A sizable number opted for the air corps, having taken the Civil Aeronautics training. At least two had joined the Royal Canadian Air Force. For the faculty, the departure of veteran teachers for other positions would include Coach Herb Klindt, Charles Martin, Guy Barnes, and Dean Joseph Pennepacker.

Among campus responses, a War Council was established, composed of both faculty and students, to deal with emergencies and cooperate fully with state and federal agencies in the war effort. In addition to counseling students on Selective Service matters, the Council would assist with civilian defense measures, promote bond and stamp sales, encourage physical fitness, support first aid and Red Cross work.

Other adjustments to wartime conditions involved eliminating classes on Monday, Wednesday, and Friday afternoons and all day Saturday so self-help students, now fewer in number, could work in the college industries and also find employment in town. With the exodus to the military and defense factories, the work force in Billings was seriously depleted. There were also some changes in the academic schedule, tightening the calendar, moving Commencement ahead a week or so.

In the wake of Pearl Harbor, there were some fears that the Japanese might strike the West Coast. That possibility prompted President

Eaton to announce that the Polytechnic stood ready to share its facilities with any damaged colleges. *The Billings Polygraph* for February 13, 1942 ventured the opinion that the Institute might be the first college in the country to offer aid to a distressed sister school. Meanwhile, Eaton reported that a new two-year curriculum would prepare young men for military service, training them in such areas as: automotive and aircraft mechanics, radio, mathematics, drafting, first aid, physical fitness, and photography.

Commencement in 1942 found 80 graduates receiving degrees, diplomas, and other certificates. There were 33 in campus programs, with 10 completing work in the four-year college. There would be no *Poly* annual to record the year's activities, due to lack of money for publication. Summer school was promoted as the opportunity for high school graduates to begin their college work in June. It was also the time for Polyites to acquire more training before being called by the military.

Unlike World War I, the Polytechnic did not convert into a military school, though there were students enrolled in the several reserve programs. Representatives of the four services, army, navy, air corps, and marines, had been on campus to meet with eligible candidates and administer the oath of enlistment. President Eaton hoped for more, for navy and air corp. cadet programs on campus, bringing in urgently needed federal dollars. The school was selected to train army aviation cadets, but the lack of funds to upgrade the facilities figured in the loss of military contracts.

Meanwhile, further evidence of wartime pressures was the dismissal of classes for one week in October, 1942 to help with the harvest. Teams were chosen to top the sugar beets, load, drive, and pile them, to dig the potatoes, to pick the tomatoes and other vegetables and can them. Recognition was duly given to the best performers in the subsequent issues of the *Polygraph*. Coach Klindt's resignation in February, 1943 after 13 years as Athletic Director added to the campus's sense of loss. Fortunately, he would return after the war, but those years had seen a dramatic reversal in the school's athletic fortunes, with a string of championships in basketball, track and field competitions.

photo by Zuck's Studio

photo by Ward McMasters

Dean Joseph Pennepacker *Herbert Klindt* *President William Copeland*

The Chapel Choir, 1939

H.M. S. Pinafore

Other evidences of wartime stringencies included a dropoff in attendance at the Candlelight Supper and a reduced version of the *Polygraph*. In athletics, baseball joined basketball in ending Conference competition due to travel costs and low male enrollment. Commencement in May, 1943 found 22 students receiving baccalaureate degrees, with another 13 diplomas.

For the faculty, there were the added responsibilities, venturing into fields left vacant, doubling in courses, with a qualified student or two pressed into service. Old faithfuls like Harry Biddinger at the Business School, now mayor of Billings, found time to teach shorthand and penmanship, while Emma Johnson managed with minimum student help in the library and bookbindery. Others deserve mention, part of an extraordinary effort, essential to survival, to see things through.

Faculty were also involved in the Institute's adult division, in evening classes aimed at the townspeople, where enrollments held steady or increased. Some participants were studying for a college degree, but most were taking a course or two of particular interest to them. Included in a range of offerings were: Art and Aviation topics, Spanish, History, the British novel, and Bible heritage. Classes were held at the new Business College location at 3rd Avenue N. and 32nd Street. Harry Biddinger had purchased the property in anticipation of acquiring the school.

It would be mistaken to picture campus life during the war years as quiet and devoid of much activity. Despite the demographics—90 per cent female by 1944— the Student Senate and a literary society or two maintained a social calendar. There were dances, picnics on the Rims, performances by the Masqued Thespians, and campus cleanup days. If intercollegiate events had been canceled, there were still tennis tournaments pitting local talent, and a skating rink south of Kenney Hall to provide wintertime enjoyment. Kimball girls also kept Postmaster Cletus Walsh busy mailing letters to boy friends at Fort Lewis and elsewhere.

The summer of 1944 brought the war especially close with the presence on campus of approximately 250 Italian prisoners of war. The employment of Mexican nationals and workers from Texas left the need for 300 or more in the area sugar beet fields. It was time for thinning operations. Agreements were reached with the Army and the Great Western Sugar Company, facilitated by the local Commercial Club, to bring in German war prisoners from a camp in Idaho. The Poly campus was seen as "an ideal" location for housing and the school's trustees agreed. It was done as a community service, "in view of the existing emergency and the immediate need for housing, and at the request of the Commercial club committees."[10]

The decision would require the moving of the summer-quarter courses in town to the Billings Business College, changing class schedules from morning to afternoons, but Dean H.A. Moore had no problem with that. Poly officials signed a lease contract for three buildings—Kenney Hall (prisoners), Tyler Hall (Army Personnel) and Prescott Commons (mess hall). Erection of barricades and floodlights around Kenney Hall provided security, along with an army guard detail. The campus was ready for the arrival of approximately 250 Italian war prisoners in early June. It had to be one of the most unusual sights ever seen by residents along Poly Drive.

Beet growers paid the government standard wages for each prisoner, working an 8 hour day. The college benefitted from rentals, though damages made to Kenney Hall may have offset the gains.[11] Unlike in Worland, Wyoming where German prisoners struck briefly, the Billings area experience with the Italians was largely uneventful, ending in late July with the completion of work in the beet fields.* Growers were generally satisfied with the wartime source of labor. It was reported that at least 400 acres of beets had been saved.[12]

The war years sorely tested the will to carry on. President Eaton wrote to "loyal friends," including previous supporters in the region and back East, stressing the school's "very critical" financial situation, noting he was determined "to keep a nucleus of the institution alive in order to make ready for those important post-war years."[13] Other correspondence concerned unmet annuity payments, bond obligations, unpaid salaries, indebtedness to merchants and so on. A beleaguered president figured that $150,000 in ready cash would clear most accounts.

---

* There was a report of one prisoner who escaped but was soon found hiding in the officers' quarters in Tyler Hall.

The George I. Alden Trust was among contributors who had terminated support, following a visit to the campus in 1943. The college was found in "too precarious" a state to justify further investment at that time. In lengthy response, Eaton answered the charges, regretting that he could not do so in person, stressing that the Polytechnic had more assets than at any time in its history, that properties could be sold to raise sufficient cash but that would weaken the school in its ability to pursue its mission.*

By 1945, however, the sale of land became essential to the Polytechnic's survival. Between October 8, 1945 and June 20, 1950 the Polytechnic Institute and its successor, Rocky Mountain College, sold what is now called the College Subdivision. There were in all 183 deed transfers, most in the Subdivision of 80 acres, with an indicated lot price of $1,000.[14] The campus at one time was reported to have 287 acres of irrigated land, with additional property at Beehive.[15] Around 110 acres remained, with the Beehive land also passing out of school ownership.[16]

ROCKY MOUNTAIN COLLEGE

Meanwhile, there were seven college graduates (1 male) in May of 1944, along with four from the academy and 14 from the Business School. Professor Arthur W. Seebart was recognized with an honorary Doctor of Divinity for his long tenure and service to the Polytechnic. Reverend Seebart had combined ministry with teaching, serving churches in Red Lodge and elsewhere, augmenting his slim and unpredictable salary at the Institute. In addition to handling Sociology and Economics, he would be remembered for his work with the debate teams.

Congregational Superintendent Cloyd H. Connor also received an honorary doctorate. He had been serving with distinction on both the Polytechnic and Intermountain Union boards, having been elected president of the latter in 1943. Connor became a main player in the move to merge both schools in a new creation—"a more permanent and strong Christian college for the northwest."[17] But it was not a

---

* Interestingly, many years later, the Trust responded favorably to a request by President Arthur DeRosier for a substantial sum to help renovate Alden Hall.

task easily accomplished, complicated by strong loyalties to different educational traditions.

From the beginning, the Eatons, the Losekamps, and other founders had envisioned a polytechnic, a place where neglected youth could receive training in the various industries of the region. Later, Lewis and Ernest did welcome a Junior College and then a four-year Liberal Arts program, but it was only another option, not a change in the nature of the Institute. So there was concern that the old would become limited or lost in the creation of the new.

Both boards in a joint session in May of 1943 voted to continue their relationship and proceed with plans for a merger. Ernest Eaton was to remain as president, while Intermountain would retain a dean who would also teach religion for both institutions. Cloyd Connor's *Diary* reflected slow going and, at times, discouragement. He noted on January 11, 1944: "Spent all day in a meeting of Intermountain Union College Board. Did much business, but wonder what it amounts to, especially in the matter of trying to merge with Billings Polytechnic."

There had been little, if any, progress by an April 25th session: "Meeting of Board of Intermountain Union College. Rather discouraging meeting. Not much hope for the future at Poly, most of them seemed to think." Connor was appointed to chair a committee to meet with church leaders around the state, with a view to expanding the conversation about Christian oriented higher education in Montana.

The spring and summer of 1946 proved to be decisive in the fortunes of the two schools. Connor felt some reassurance in the election of several new members to the Polytechnic board, leadership types who could make a difference. The merger, it was felt, involved the search for a new president, which brought results in late July with the election of Dr. William D. Copeland of Lake Forest College in Illinois. Ernest Eaton's retirement appeared in *The Billings Gazette* on August 15, 1946. He was named President Emeritus.

The announcement of Dr. Copeland's election came two days later, with beginning date of September 1. A native Coloradan, he had degrees from Colorado College in Greeley and had done graduate study at Harvard and the University of Chicago. He held two honorary doctorates. Copeland had served Lincoln College in Illinois from 1935 to 1944, when he moved to Lake Forest College as its vice-president.

Married with three children, he was "enthusiastic over the opportunity to build at Billings a strong, fully-accredited four-year college under positive Christian influences."[18]

Dr. Copeland came at a time when returning veterans figured prominently in larger enrollments. Fortified with their G.I. Bill of Rights, they numbered 175 out of 379 students registered for the winter quarter of 1946–47. That total included 115 in the Business College and 54 in the evening program. Accommodations for married veterans had been acquired through the Federal Housing Authority in Spokane, consisting of 35 units located in the northwest corner of the campus. "Vets Village" was soon an integral part of Polytechnic life, its "All Stars" providing strong competition for the Alden and Tyler Clubs in the Campus Conference Intramurals.

The fall of 1946 also brought a familiar figure back to the campus, when Herb Klindt resumed his role as Athletic Director. The Crusaders would transition into the Rocky Bears and become again Conference contenders. Other veterans to return to the new school included Dean Joseph Pennepacker and Professor Charles Martin. Reverend Guy Barnes, who had helped shepherd the campus industries, had moved to the University Congregational Church in Missoula and opted to remain in the ministry.

Throughout the fall and winter of 1946–47 both boards worked closely on the details of a merger. Further negotiations proved necessary, but by April of 1947 the two schools were ready to become one. At a two-day meeting on the 9th and 10th of that month the critical vote was taken, with the merger to become effective on July 15, 1947. It was understood that the new institution would retain the "Open Door" policy, while seeking needed support from the three affiliated denominations: Methodist, Presbyterian, and Congregational Christian. Beyond those faith communions, however, there was hope for a larger Protestant representation, that beneath the Rims there might evolve "a great Christian College for the Rocky Mountain area."[19]

The question of a name for the new institution of higher learning produced several suggestions by the governing board, such as the College of the Yellowstone. Happily, the students had a better idea, supported it with numerous signatures on a petition and offered it to the new president. Dr. Copeland was impressed and so were the trustees and thus Rocky Mountain College came to be.

Ernest Eaton had hoped that returning veterans would fill the college's classrooms and dormitories, paving the way for future growth. He was, after all, the last of the founders who had had visions of a university beneath the Rims and that dream died hard. Polytechnic-Intermountain had enrolled over 1,000 students just before the war, though many were downtown in the Business College. But a return to such numbers was not to be, as the new institution would struggle to register between 200 and 300 during the 1950s.

There would be times, as in earlier years, when a worried president or board chair would wonder about opening in the fall. That story, however, belongs with a future volume on the Rocky Mountain College years. The College will be better, though, for a heritage of struggle and caring, for a courageous journey in faith and purpose over nearly 70 years. It will be stronger for the witness of those who matched their sorrows with their joys of believing in their work with youth, one in which they felt truly at home.

Epilogue

The story of the College's predecessor institutions brings to mind another time in the annals of American higher education. It involved the Dartmouth College Case of 1818 and, in simplest terms, the attempt to convert it from a private to a public institution. Chief Justice John Marshall presided at the trial.

Daniel Webster, class of 1801, led the defense for his alma mater, opposed by an array of brilliant attorneys employed by the State. He was still in private practice in Boston, with his fame yet in the making, but all the promise was there in an impassioned and successful five-hour presentation.

When the time came to conclude his case, under great emotional stress, felt even by the hardened lawyers and justices present, he spoke those words to Chief Justice Marshall that are remembered to this day. "It is, sir, as I have said, a small college, and yet there are those who love it."

So it was in Deer Lodge where the bells first announced higher education in Montana Territory, in Helena where a solitary building in the valley symbolized bright hopes for the future, and in Billings where a beet field became the campus for a school that, through years of trial, simply refused to die. In each case, a dedicated corps of founders, teachers, students, alumni and supporters shared enthusiasm for a venture that mattered—an open door to life and learning for the youth of a vast, inland empire.

Their legacy of caring is a courageous journey to a place called Rocky Mountain College, informed by its past, challenged by the present, alert to the inevitable changes in tomorrow's world. It was the same Daniel Webster who wrote in later years: "Those who do not look upon themselves as a link connecting the past with the future do not perform their duty to the world." So the torch is passed to each new generation, to value what abides in our college's traditions, remembering always, as Webster once put it, "It is, sir, as I have said, a small school, but there are those who love it."

Students entering the administration building of the newly formed Rocky Mountain College, 1948.

END NOTES

The references for this study consist mainly of primary sources—college publications, church journals and records, contemporary newspaper articles, manuscripts, correspondence and other unpublished materials. Unless otherwise indicated, they are found in the Methodist Archives (MA) or College Archives (CA) in the College's Educational Resource Center.

In addition, oral history has provided helpful insights and some anecdotal content. Surviving graduates of Montana Wesleyan, Intermountain Union, and the Billings Polytechnic Institute represent a significant resource, which this study has had the opportunity to tap only in small measure.

PROLOGUE ❀

1. *Powell County Where It All Began* (Deer Lodge: Powell County Museum and Art Foundation, 1959), 132.

2. George Lubick, "Cornelius Hedges, Frontier Educator," *Montana: The Magazine of Western History*, Spring, 1978, 26ff. See also Summer Issue 1975.

3. William Warren Sweet, *The Story of Religion in America* (New York and London: Harper & Brothers, 1939), 488.

4. *Journal of the First Session of the Montana Annual Conference of the Methodist Episcopal Church Held at Bozeman, Montana Territory, August 2–3, 1877.* M.A.

5. Correspondence, Mrs. Ella (Irvine) Mountjoy to M.G. Burlingame, May 14, 1942, Montana State Historical Library.

6. James Bryce, *The American Commonwealth* Vol. II. (London and New York: MacMillan and Co., 1888), 552.

CHAPTER ONE ❀

1. *Jordan Tribune*, n.d., Deer Lodge file, Montana Room, Parmly Billings Library, Billings.

2. *The Philipsburg Mail*, n.d., Deer Lodge file, Montana Room, Parmly Billings Library, Billings.

3. *Powell County Where It All Began*, 122.

4. *Ibid*, 132.

5. *The New North-West*, Deer Lodge, July 5, 1878. Articles in this newspaper followed with interest developments with the local college.

6. Dan Baum, "Butte America," *American Heritage*, April 1997. Butte's population crested in 1917 when the city directory listed more than 96,000 residents.

7. *The New North-West*, February 22, 1878.

8. *Ibid.*, February 14, 1878. Deer Lodge was also the scene for Roman Catholic efforts in education. Fr. Remigius de Ryckere was joined by the Sisters of Charity of Leavenworth, Kansas in 1878 in establishing St. Mary's Academy for girls. Work continued on a building for three years, with the official opening on September 4, 1882.

News of educational developments in Deer Lodge seems to have circulated rather widely, for *The New North-West* on July 5, 1878 reported an item from the *Salt Lake Tribune*: "Deer Lodge is to be the university town of Montana."

9. *The Weekly Miner*, Butte, October 1, 1878.

10. Ella Mountjoy-Burlingame Correspondence.

11. *The New North-West*, December 13, 1878.

12. *Ibid.*, April 25, 1879.

13. Wiley Mountjoy-Burlingame Correspondence, May 14, 1942, Montana State Historical Library.

14. Merrill G. Burlingame and Harvey C. Hartling, *Big Sky Disciples* (Great Falls: Christian Church of Montana, 1984) provides information about Mountjoy's career.

15. *The New North-West*, February 24, 1882.

16. Colin B. Goodykoontz, *Home Missions on the American Frontier With Particular Reference to the American Home Missionary Society* (Caldwell, Idaho: Caxton Printers, Ltd., 1939), 394.

17. Duncan J. McMillan file, Presbyterian Historical Library, Philadelphia.

18. *The New North-West*, August 25, 1882.

19. McMillan file.

20. George Edwards, *The Pioneer Work of the Presbyterian Church In Montana* (Helena: Independent Publishing Co., n.d.), 121 ff.

CHAPTER TWO ❋

1. Helen Fitzgerald Sanders, *A History of Montana*, Vol. I (Chicago and New York: Lewis Publishing Company, 1913), 527.

2. Edwards, 151.

3. *College of Montana Catalogue*, Deer Lodge, 1883–84, 19, CA.

4. Goodykoontz, 395.

5. McMillan File.

6. *Ibid.*

7. Bryce, 568.

8. McMillan—S.T. Hauser Correspondence, October 1887, Montana State Historical Library.

9. McMillan File.

10. *Ibid.*

11. Sanders, I., 577.

12. Bryce, 566–7.

13. Edwards, 124.

CHAPTER THREE ❋

1. Lewis T. Eaton, "Personal Story," a manuscript recollection of the Deer Lodge years and the beginnings of the Billings Polytechnic Institute, CA.

2. *Ibid.*

3. *Second Annual Announcement of Montana College, 1905–6*, Deer Lodge, CA.

4. *Ibid.*

5. Eaton.

6. Merrill G. Burlingame and K. Ross Toole, eds., *A History of Montana*, Vol. III (New York: Lewis Historical Publishing Co., 1957) 403–4.

7. Margaret Mountjoy, "Story of College of Montana," manuscript recollection, 4, CA.

8. Eaton.

9. Bryce, 553.

10. June Getchell, "Deer Lodge pools historic educational functions," n.d. article, Deer Lodge file, Montana Room, Parmly Billings Library.

11. Sanders, I, 577.

12. Ernest Eaton also recalled that the campus had been reduced to 11 acres.

13. This is the figure also reported in the merger articles creating Rocky Mountain College.

CHAPTER FOUR ❈

1. Paul M. Adams, "History of Montana Wesleyan and Intermountain Union College," Methodist Archives, R.M.C., 3. This lengthy manuscript, typed and undated, is a valuable recollection by one who shared intimately in the lives of the two colleges from early years.

2. *Minutes, Montana Annual Conference of the Methodist Episcopal Church, 1887*, 28, MA.

3. *Ibid.*

4. Adams, 7. See also Fred Gamer manuscript article, April, 1910, MA.

5. Paul M. Adams, *When Wagon Trails Were Dim* (Helena: Montana Conference Board of Education, 1957) 66.

6. *Minutes*, 1889, 70.

7. *Ibid.*, 34.

8. Adams, "History," 7.

9. Edward Laird Mills, "The Past, Present and Future of the Montana Wesleyan University," manuscript article, MA.

10. Gamer, 1.

11. *Minutes*, 1891, 22.

12. Adams, "History," 8.

13. *Ibid.*

14. *Minutes*, 1892, 53-54.

15. Adams, "History," 11.

16. "A Brief Account of the Third Anniversary Exercises of the Montana University," pamphlet, Helena, MT., June 11–14, 1893, 55, CA.

17. Adams, "History," 22.

18. *Ibid.*, See Adams, *Wagon Trails*, 55 PF for more on Mills.

19. *Ibid.*, 24.

20. *Ibid.*, 26.

21. *Official Journal of the Montana Annual Conference*, 1902, 49, MA.

22. *The Bulletin of Intermountain Union College*, August, 1932, 2, CA.

23. *Official Journal*, 1903, 48.

24. *Official Journal*, 1905, 48–49.

25. Adams, "History," 52.

26. Marjorie Buhl, *History of Higher Education in Montana, 1883–1958* (Billings: Rocky Mountain College, 1958), 9. This is a brief discussion of the college's predecessor institutions.

27. *Official Journal*, 1905, 49.

28. *Ibid.*, 49–52.

29. Adams, "History," 48.

30. "President's Report on Montana Wesleyan University, 1907–1908," *University Bulletin*, Vol. I, No. I, 11, CA.

31. Edward Laird Mills, *Plains, Peaks and Pioneers* (Portland, Oregon: Binfords & Mort, 1947), 159.

32. Adams, "History," 61.

33. *Official Journal*, 1911, 34–35.

CHAPTER FIVE ❈

1. Adams, "History," 57.

2. "Montana Wesleyan University," *Campaign Bulletin*, No. 3, November, 1913, MA.

3. Edward L. Mills, "Montana Wesleyan—The Duty of the Hour," manuscript article, 3, MA.

4. *Ibid*, 2.

5. *Prickly Pear*, 1914–15, 34. A student publication, this Wesleyan Annual was a creditable record of campus life.

6. Mills, 1.

7. Adams, 70.

8. *Prickly Pear*, 1915–16, 8.

9. Adams, 77.

10. *Ibid*.

11. *Official Journal*, 1917, 105.

12. *Ibid*, 1919, 289.

13. Adams, 91.

14. *Ibid*, 93.

15. *Official Journal*, 1921, 107.

16. *Montana Wesleyan College Annual Report*, August 25, 1922, 1–2, MA.

17. *Montana Wesleyan College Announcement*, February 5, 1923, 7. MA.

18. *Official Journal*, 1920, 48-9.

19. Lawrence F. Small, ed., *Religion in Montana*, Vol. II (Billings: Rocky Mountain College, 1995), see Chapter VI.

20. *Minutes of the Synod of Montana*, 1921, 37, CA.

21. Lawrence F. Small, *Trails Revisited, The Story of the Montana-Northern Wyoming Conference*, U.C.C. (Billings: Conference, 1998), 64ff.

22. *Historical Statement Concerning Intermountain Union College*, February, 1924, 5. I.C.U. file, CA.

23. *Ibid*, 8.

24. *Montana Record-Herald*, Helena, August 29, 1923.

25. *Historical Statement*, 9. See for full text of the merger plan.

26. *Montana Record-Herald*, September 3, 1923.

27. *Annual Catalogue, Intermountain Union College*, 1924–25, 12, CA.

28. *Ibid*, 12–13.

29. *Montana Record-Herald*, September 17, 1923.

30. *Historical Statement*, 17.

CHAPTER SIX

1. *Prickly Pear*, 1925, n.p.

2. Adams, "History," MA, 102.

3. Mills, *Plains*, 162.

4. Adams, 108.

5. *The Bulletin of I.U.C.*, November 1926, 3.

6. Adams, 108.

7. *Bulletin*, 1.

8. Adams, 104.

9. *Bulletin*, November, 1929, 7.

10. *Ibid*, 3.

11. *Ibid*, 11.

12. Adams, 115.

13. Mills, 163.

14. Adams, 121.

15. *Ibid*, 126.

16. Mills, 165.

CHAPTER SEVEN ❖

1. Lawrence F. Small, *A Century of Politics on the Yellowstone* (Billings: Rocky Mountain College, 1983), 21.

2. *The Billings Gazette*, June 26, 1908.

3. Lawrence F. Small, "Preston B. Moss and the Billings Polytechnic Institute," Billings Preservation File, Montana Room, Parmly Billings Library.

4. *Bulletin*, Billings Polytechnic Institute, Vol. 1, No. 1, September 1, 1908, 4, CA.

5. Eaton, "Personal Story."

6. Small, *Trails*, 64.

7. Lewis Eaton correspondence, January 22, 1909, CA.

8. "What Others Say About the Polytechnic," pamphlet, CA.

9. Eaton correspondence, January 23, 1909, CA.

10. *Ibid*, February 21, 1909.

11. Eaton, "Personal Story," 13.

12. Ethel Bean Storm correspondence, December 21, 1971, CA.

13. *The Billings Polygraph*, January 24, 1929, CA. An incomplete file of this campus newspaper still provides valuable information on life at the Polytechnic.

14. Eaton, "Personal Story."

15. "It Can Be Done," pamphlet, Poly File, Montana Room, Parmly Billings Library.

16. Billings Board of Trade correspondence, CA.

17. *Ibid*.

18. *The Poly*, 1912, 38. This annual was a major publication, providing a pictorial and other record of life at the Polytechnic.

19. *Polytechnic Bulletin*, January, 1913, 3.

20. *Ibid.*

21. *The Silver State*, Deer Lodge, July 19, 1917.

CHAPTER EIGHT ❖

1. *Polytechnic Bulletin*, January, 1913, 3.

2. *Ibid.*, January 1914, 3.

3. *Ibid.*, March, 1934, 3.

4. Willis E. Lougee, *A Retrospect*, unpub. manuscript 40, CA.

5. "Report of Mr. Willis E. Lougee," 1914, pamphlet, CA.

6. *Billings Daily Tribune*, September 29, 1914, 1, 8.

7. *Ibid.*, October 14, 1914, 1, 8.

8. *Ibid.*, October 14, 8.

9. Small, *Century*, 61.

10. *The Polygraph*, May 27, 1919, 21.

11. Lougee, 42.

12. Lougee, 41.

13. *The Billings Polygraph*, January 17, 1928, 1.

14. *Ibid.*, December 19, 1929.

15. *Polytechnic Bulletin*, November, 1930, 4.

16. "Beehive Camp," brochure, undated, CA.

17. *The Poly*, 1933, 93.

18. *The Billings Polygraph*, January 12, 1934, 1, 4.

19. *Ibid.*, 4.

CHAPTER NINE 🏵

1. *The Billings Polygraph*, 1935

2. *Ibid.*, October 21, 1936.

3. Small, *Trails*, 131.

4. *The Billings Polygraph*, April, 1938.

5. *The Billings Gazette*, February 27, 1938.

6. "An Explanation of the Polytechnic Campaign to Secure $1,250,000," promotional brochure, Eaton papers, CA.

7. *The Billings Polygraph*, June 7, 1940.

8. *Ibid.*, February 21, 1941.

9. *Ibid.*, May 23, 1941.

10. *Gazette*, May 28, 1944.

11. "The agreement with the War Department, signed June 1, 1944," document, Eaton papers, CA.

12. *Gazette*, July 28, 1944.

13. Eaton correspondence, form letter to donors, undated, Eaton papers, CA.

14. Deed Record Books, Yellowstone County Clerk of Records, Nos. 5 and 6.

15. *Gazette*, June 4, 1933.

16. Correspondence with Alden Trust, April 15, 1944, Eaton papers, CA.

17. Small, *Trails*, 132.

18. *Ibid.*, 138. See Copeland correspondence with Messrs. Adams, Doolen, and Hammerstrom, June–August, 1946, for details concerning his coming to Billings and the challenge of the college's precarious financial condition. Copeland papers, CA.

19. *Polygraph*, April 15, 1947.

Poly Drive in 1939.

$\mathcal{I}$NDEX